only bob

Thanks, Brenda.
God bless.
bob Marlowe

by Bob Marlowe

only bob
Copyright © 2019 by Bob Marlowe

only bob / Bob Marlowe
First Edition

ACKNOWLEDGEMENTS

First, I would like to thank Katharine (Kathy) Newton for standing beside me through this book writing adventure. Your support, time, advice, encouragement, and most of all patience was invaluable to me… Without Kathy this book would not be possible. I would not want a better friend than Kathy.

Many thanks to Jason and Heather Barr of Revival Creatives for the pictures, layout, and editing. You worked tirelessly… that is why you are the best. My best to you.

Also, many thanks to my family and friends for providing the basis of all these stories and for putting up with me all these years.

ABOUT THE AUTHOR

Bob was born and reared in Newton, N. C.. After high school graduation he enlisted in the Navy, serving two voluntary tours in Vietnam. After receiving his Honorable Discharge, he attended Central Piedmont Community College in Charlotte where he was a member of Phi Theta Kappa, the National Honor Society for Junior Colleges. Bob retired from the furniture industry as a Purchasing Agent. Bob resides in Claremont, N. C. on his 100 acre farm with his wife Gaye and plenty of dogs and cows. Bob can be reached at bemarlowe@embarqmail. com.

To Gaye and Justin

The greatest joy of my life is being your husband and father. Thanks for traveling the journey of this thing called life with me.

TABLE OF CONTENTS

SMALL TOWN LIVIN'

FLAG OWNERS

My Dad died in 1982. He was a WWII vet and an American Patriot who loved America, its way of life, and the opportunities available to us. As you can imagine we had a military funeral for him with the rifle salute, taps, and a large American flag on his casket. During the service, someone folded the flag and presented it to Mom on behalf of a "grateful nation." I loved that flag and wanted it very badly, but I hesitated to ask Mom. In late June of 1983, Mom called me and told me I could have that flag if I would buy a flag pole and fly it every July 4.

At the time there were no flag companies in this county and of course no internet to locate one. I remembered a company called Conger Flag Company in Charlotte located in front of the old Krispy Kreme. On Saturday morning I drove the 50 miles to Charlotte, selected the pole that I wanted… but there was a problem. I had left my wallet at home. I had no money, no credit card, and couldn't even prove who I was. The man at the flag company told me not to fret over it. He said to take that pole home, install it, and fly the flag. He said, "You can mail me a check." I said, "You don't even know who I am, I could tell you anything." He affirmed to me that "people who buy flag poles pay their bills." I mailed the check as soon as I got home. I even took it to the post office so he would get it in Monday's mail. If I come by your home and see a flag flying, you can bet that I trust you. I'm convinced that he was right in saying, "people who buy flag poles pay their bills." God Bless you all and God Bless America. bob

THE SUIT

There was a time in my life when I would wear a suit from time to time. I'm glad those days are gone. About forty years ago as we were leaving church, I noticed that my father-in-law was wearing a suit just like I had been wanting. It was a beige/khaki type suit. At lunch, I was asking him about it. He said it came from a store in Valdese for $59.95. He said the store sold "seconds and irregulars" but he didn't find a thing wrong with his. That was a good buy. Being a newly-wed I didn't have much money so I decided I could probably afford one. My father-in-law said he would take me up there next week because he would like to get another one.

The following Saturday, He, my mother-in-law, and Gaye and I went up there. I immediately found a suit just like his. We examined it and found no flaws. The coat fit perfectly and I went into the dressing room and the waist size was perfect. My mother-in-law said she would hem the pants for me and I could wear them to church the next day. I told her to hem them to 32". She hurriedly hemmed them and told me to try them on to make sure she measured right.

I put them on and they were about 15" too long. She remeasured the pants and they were 32". We didn't know what was wrong with them. I put them back on and they were what I would call "long crotched." The crotch was below my knees. I said that "I guess I could use the coat as a sport coat and throw the pants away since the store had a no return policy." My father-in-law said, "No, let's just hem them to the proper length." I told him, "No, they would look like Barnum and Bailey pants." If she would have hemmed them they would have been size 36 waist and 9" length. bob

BISCUITS

We don't have many rules around here. I have two rules for Gaye and she has two rules for me. I'm not allowed to pee off the porch and I must leave muddy boots on the porch. I have no idea why she has the rule about peeing. I think she saw that once in a western movie.

My two rules for her is all chicken must have bones and NO CANNED BISCUITS. A couple of weeks ago she came in with some canned biscuits. I immediately headed to the phone to call our attorney, John Cilley, to start divorce proceedings, but she stopped me. We've been married forty-two years without canned biscuits and no need to start now in my opinion. She explained to me that they were on sale for ten cents a can at Honey's and she just couldn't resist. I kinda understand that. She put them in the refrigerator and they have been there since.

Yesterday we heard something go "pop." A can of them had burst open on their own in the refrigerator so we baked them. I put on a sour face and tried to act indignant toward them to ensure that she didn't think I liked them. It's not likely that she thinks I didn't like them though. I ate about 4 of them and then today I ate a couple more with a tomato slice on it. It's hard to beat a day-old biscuit with a slice of tomato on it...... even if it is canned biscuits. Please don't tell Gaye that I liked them because I don't want it to become a habit with her. bob

MAMA SLEDDING

Well, it is starting to sleet some here in the Catawba Valley. According to my weather app, it is supposed to last until about 6PM. I have finished all my outdoor work and am safely in the house.

I'm reminded about my early life when we had snow. I lived on a hill on S Main Avenue in Newton between J Street and Hwy 321, which was a great hill for sledding. People from all over town would come to sled on that hill. We would sled there for a while and then go to Oakland Circle in Dogwood Hills, another great hill for sledding. We would sled until midnight or later. I'll never forget the night Mom made a big pot of hot chocolate for us kids and brought it out to us. It was the real thing made on the stove with real milk, cocoa, and sugar…not that instant stuff people now use. Mom got the idea she wanted to sled with us and did so for probably 30 minutes. I was embarrassed by that little episode, but everyone thought she was the coolest thing on the hill.

That's now a fond memory of such a sweet woman who loved all the kids in the neighborhood. bob

THE DOUBLE COLA MAN

When I was seven years old in the early 50's Double Cola was my favorite drink. We rarely had them because Dad thought there was nothing like the 6 oz Cokes. To promote their product, the "Double Cola Man" would walk the streets and stop at random houses and he would give you a silver dollar for every DC that you had. When he was in the area, the phone lines got hot to alert everyone.

In those days, it was common for kids to stay alone while their parents were at work. Dad kept fifty cents in his dresser for my sister and me to use in an emergency, and I considered this an emergency. I ran to Pop Reitzel's Store and bought 12 DCs. In the meantime, Dad got home from work and was not a happy camper. While he was fussing at me, there was a knock on the door and it was the "DC Man." Dad got happy when he received 12 silver dollars. Dad gave me one and it was the first dollar I ever had. I spent it all the next day while Dad and Mom were at work.

This is just another happy remembrance of my childhood. bob

REMEMBERING DAD

Father's Day is almost here and I have been thinking about my Dad for the past few days.

Dad was a solemn type of fellow without much to say. He rarely came forth with many endearing words. That was common for men of his era. He was most famous for, "Bobby, go get me a hickory." For you young readers, a "hickory" was a stick to whip me with.

Although Dad never used the word "love" we knew he loved us. His way of showing love was to keep us fed, a roof over our heads, and clean clothes on our backs... That was also common for men of his era. He also showed his love by having a pretty strict set of rules for us to go by. He expected us to be courteous, polite, go to school even when we were sick, and to show respect to our elders. For the most part, I followed those rules.

He also had rules like, "squeeze the toothpaste from the bottom and roll it up as you go." I often had trouble with that rule. It seemed to me you would get the same amount of toothpaste out no matter where you squeezed. Also, when you got through sweeping, put the broom in the corner where it belongs with the handle on the floor and the brush part on top. A broom would last longer like that? I don't know, but those disciplines helped me in later life.

Dad believed in shaking hands. His handshake and his word were his bond. A handshake to him meant, "nice to meet you," or "it's a deal," etc. During my two tours in Vietnam, Dad and Mom would see me off at the airport and greet me upon my return. Mom and I would hug and say our byes, and Dad would stand erect and shake my hand. I knew that was his way of telling me that he loved me.

In February of 1982, Dad got cancer and spent the next 6 months either at home or the VA Hospital in Oteen, NC. I would drive the 85 or so miles every day after work to see him. Mom always went along and we had a lot of time to talk during those trips.

On one of those trips, Dad told us that the preacher from First Baptist Church in Newton had been there and he accepted the Lord for the first time. He always went to church and I just assumed he had been saved. He said it happened "in the twinkling of an eye."

On October 1, the doctor told us that Dad only had a week to 10 days to live. As we were leaving that day, Dad told Mom that he loved her. Then with a pause and almost as an afterthought, he said, "I love you too, Bobby." We embraced for the first time and he died on October 3...... 2 days later. He finally said the words that I had always longed to hear.

You know, Mama showed us how to love, and Dad, in his own slow way, taught us to express it often.

Thanks, for indulging me. bob

THE SECOND GREATEST LOVE

The greatest love is the love of God. I think the second greatest love is a mother's love of a child… that maternal instinct.

Yesterday I moved the cows to their winter grazing and to prepare them for calving season, which is scheduled to begin October 9th. When I got up this morning, a cow was out and running around in the yard. I got her back in the pasture and she got out two more times and was wildly running around, bawling and foaming at the mouth. I finally got the idea that her calf had been born prematurely and was still in the summer pasture. Gaye got the idea to put the cow back in summer pasture and if she did have a calf, she would find it. When I got her in the summer pasture, she was running around with her nose to the ground trying to pick up the scent of her calf. She finally found it and mother and daughter are doing well.

Today, I am thankful for mothers and for being blessed to live this lifestyle. I get to witness God's grace every day.

I'm also thankful for a mother who never gave up on me. bob

THE BEATLES

When I was a junior in high school in 1963, it was common that most girls had to be home from a date at 11PM. Our parents gave the boys a little more freedom. Most of us had to be home by midnight.

It was also common for my friends and I to meet after our dates in the parking lot of the Harris Teeter Grocery Store on North Main Avenue in Newton, NC. We would sometimes just stand around and compare stories and sometimes we would go riding around town.

On this night, we decided to ride around in one of the guy's Chevy convertible. It was freezing cold, but we put the top down and turned on the heater, which didn't really help me because I was sitting in the middle of the back seat.

The radio station in our home town signed off at 11PM. If we wanted to hear music after 11PM, we would listen to WOWO in Fort Wayne, Indiana or sometimes KDKA in Pittsburg. My favorite was WLS in Chicago. Those 50,000-watt clear channel AM stations could reach 30 or 40 states and parts of Canada.

Now back to my story. Dick Biondi was the DJ on WLS that we all liked. He was quite controversial and did and said things that other DJs would not dare to do or say. He was ahead of his time.

On this particular night, we were about a block down the road from the Harris Teeter when the tube-type car radio warmed up and suddenly we heard a sound unlike anything we had ever heard coming out of those speakers. Everyone in the car got quiet and we listened to this unique song...... and even more unique singing group. It was the Beatles. I believe the song was, "Please, Please Me" but I am not sure. It could have been, "I Want to Hold Your Hand." I simply cannot remember.

Dick Biondi was the only DJ in America who was playing the Beatles, and the five of us in that Chevy were the first from our school to hear it. Rock and roll music changed forever on that night. I still love the rock and roll from that era, but I am not too much on the pathetic stuff being played today. Today I prefer Classic Country and Southern Gospel. bob

GROWING OLD

As you grow older, it seems that you lose a lot of things. No, I'm not talking about personal possessions, but other more important things.

Many people of my age speak of losing their memory. Yep, I have that problem. I can remember things from long ago, but somehow forget events that happened in recent years. If I think long enough, I can usually pull it out of my memory bank.

I heard a doctor say recently that many senior citizens think they have dementia of some type, but most do not. Actually, people of my age have seen so many changes, and we have so much stored in our brains that it is often hard to retrieve it. Hopefully, some of you will feel better about yourself by knowing that.

The thing I miss most is my loss of smell. Actually, I can still smell, but everything smells the same. It doesn't matter if I am in the men's room at Hickory Motor Speedway or a fine restaurant......it all smells the same. I was given a nasal spray by my ENT doctor a few years ago, and one of the side effects was "altered smell." I no longer use that spray, but I still have altered smell. It just never did go away.

I like to smell things and sure do miss it; i.e. the smell of a pie baking in the oven, the scent of flowers and blooming trees, a fine perfume, and the sweet, warm aroma of my mother etc. For those of you who do not live in the country, you actually learn to like the aroma of freshly mowed hay in a barn mingled with the smell of cow manure. You don't understand, I know.

When I stepped off the plane at Tan Son Nhut airport on my first trip to Vietnam, the first thing I noticed was the stench in the air and the sweltering heat. The whole country had the same odor. You grow used to it, and do not even notice after a while. It may seem odd to you, but somehow, I can still smell that stench in my imagination. bob

WEDDING DAY

Goodness, I have been thinking. Next week we will be celebrating our wedding anniversary. Where has the time gone? Although I can't remember what happened last week, I'll never forget Saturday afternoon, June 20, 1970. It was a wonderful day.

I remember standing behind the church with my Dad waiting to make our grand entrance for the ceremony. We were just chit-chatting about whatever came to our minds. I'll never forget that my Dad asked, "How much do you pay the preacher?" I told him, "I didn't know you were supposed to pay the preacher." I couldn't afford to pay him anyway. You see, I had less than $100 and that was for our honeymoon. When I told Dad my financial situation, he said he would pay the preacher for me. I sure did appreciate that.

The last thing I asked Dad before we went in for the ceremony is, "What advice do you have for me?" He thought for a moment and said, "Take her to church every Sunday and base your standard of living on one income because you never know when one of you will get sick or lose your job." That was good advice and we have followed that advice to this day.

After the wedding, we went to Gaye's parent's house to get ready for our two-day honeymoon to Pigeon Forge. In those days, the bride put on "traveling clothes" which usually consisted of a nice dress with a corsage. I didn't know about getting dressed up for travel... I put on a pair of shorts and flip flops. When I came out dressed like that, someone (who will remain nameless) jumped all over me and said, "You can't travel like that." I told her that was, "the best I had except for the suit that I had rented and it had to be returned by Monday morning or I would have to pay more money, which I didn't have." She said, "Let me look in your suitcase." I told her that I didn't have a suitcase. I had packed my clothes in a Winn-Dixie grocery bag. With her pious nose stuck up in the air, she grabbed that bag, dumped it on the bed, and saw that I was telling the truth. I never did particularly care for her from that day forward. I ended up putting my wedding suit back on and wearing that.

While we were on our two-day honeymoon in Pigeon Forge, we went to see the country music duo, Bonnie Lou and Buster. Pigeon Forge was not a vacation destination at the time, and there just wasn't much to do. We came home on Monday morning because the money was almost gone.

Those were wonderful days that seemed hard at the time, but we worked through it and ended up making something of ourselves. It has been a great ride. bob

MISCHIEF

I was feeling a little mischievous today. I got the pole position at Walmart. Yes sir, there I was in the first parking spot near the door. After buying a dog collar and leash for the new dog, I was walking back to the car. There was a mean-looking fellow driving up who wanted my parking spot so he stopped and was waiting for me to back out. The way this mean-looking fellow's forehead sloped down to his jaws and nose, and the way his ears were sticking out, he reminded me of a 40 Ford Coupe with the doors open. I didn't want that "mean-looking guy who reminded me of a 40 Ford Coupe with the doors open" to have my parking spot. To have a little fun with him, I got in my car, started it up, put it in reverse so the back-up lights would be on and I just sat there. The first thing you know there was a traffic jam that would remind you of something you would see in New York City. NEW YORK CITY!!! Anyway, with all the cars backed up behind him, he got frustrated and moved on. I quickly backed out so that the old couple in the car behind him could get my space. I should be ashamed of myself. NOT. bob

GRANDMA'S GRITS

I woke up this morning in the mood for grits... just a bowl of grits, no egg, no bacon, no toast... just grits.

People eat grits in all sorts of ways. Some people add butter or cheese to them and that is good. I sometimes eat them with eggs and mix the grits with the eggs. I'll never forget the first time we had grits at the Navy Recruit Training Center in Great Lakes, Illinois. Some of the northern boys ate them with milk and sugar, just like oatmeal. That totally confused me until I found out that they didn't know what grits are. They thought it was farina, which I believe is Cream of Wheat, but not sure. For me, I prefer my grits with a lot of pepper and a couple dashes of Texas Pete hot sauce.

I used to love to spend the night with Grandpa and Grandma Sims when I was a mere lad of about eight years. Grandpa and I would rise before daylight and milk his two jersey cows. I remember how cold my hands would get. I sure did look forward to getting back to the house for a hot breakfast. Breakfast was always ready as soon as we entered the door...

Grandma was only an average cook... maybe below average, but I am comparing it to Mom's which was top notch. Grandma Sims' grits were always dry and lumpy, but their taste was exquisite. I'm not sure, but I believe she didn't stir them as often as necessary or maybe just cooked them too long. They were not a pretty sight, but you can't judge a book by the cover. I often thought they would make good catfish bait. They might not have been pretty, but they were the best tasting grits I had ever eaten until this day. I believe her secret was the bacon and sausage grease that she mixed with them.

This reminds me that beauty is only skin deep. Some of the nicest people I know are as ugly as Grandma's grits, but their friendship to me is a beautiful thing. Try not to judge people… just accept them. bob

MAMA'S BIRTHDAY

Age is an interesting topic. I never thought much about age until I turned 65 and started Social Security. For some reason at that age you become a "senior citizen." It seems just like yesterday when I was in high school, and 3 years later I was in Vietnam. Gaye and I have been married for 48 years and it only seems like 10 years ago. Time flies when you're having fun….and to be honest, most of my life has been based on fun more than anything else. I still have fun, but I do know what is important these days.

Mama never liked to talk about her age. I think that is true of most women, but Mama was extreme in her thinking.

In 1969, Gaye and I were dating and we took her a birthday cake and a few gifts for her birthday. We had a good time at our little party, but after it was over Mama said we needed to have a little talk. She said, "I don't like to celebrate birthdays, especially my own. After all, I didn't have anything to do with it." She said she didn't want any more birthday parties.

Well, we quit buying her birthday cakes, gifts, and cards from that day forward. We would go to her house about a week after her birthday and tell her we were thinking about her and thought, "She just might like these little gifts." We never said the words, "Happy Birthday." That would have been suicide.

Mom didn't like anything about being old. When my hair started turning white in my early 30's, Mom said, "If you start dying it now before it turns completely white, no one will ever know the difference, but if you wait everyone will know." She wasn't all that happy with me when I told her I was just going to let nature take its course and whatever happened would be how it would stay. The truth is she didn't want anyone to know that she had a white-haired son. She soon got over it.

You know, Mom always looked and acted young. There must be some truth to her thoughts. After all, age is just a number. bob

TRICK OR TREAT

Halloween is coming up in a few weeks. I really did enjoy Halloween as a kid, but not so much now.

When I was in elementary school, we always had a Fall festival with a chicken and dumpling supper. Every kid in the school had tickets to sell for this meal, and they went fast. After the meal, all of the children would go trick or treating.

I remember the first time I went trick or treating. I was about five and my sister was eight.

Mama dressed me up in one of my sister's dresses, put lipstick and rouge on my face, and an old wig on my head. I went as a girl, and my sister put an old sheet over her head and went as a ghost.

I was quite naïve at that age (still am at this age), and all I knew was that you went from door to door saying, "trick or treat" and people gave you candy. We were getting a lot of candy and having a good time.

The last house we stopped at was Horace Henderson's house on North Davis Avenue. We said, "trick or treat," and Mr. Henderson responded with, "trick." My sister and I looked at one another with unsure eyes. Mr. and Mrs. Henderson laughed uncontrollably as I stood on my head and my sister did the split. Those were the only tricks we knew… we did get candy though.

I still do not understand things. bob

IMAGINATION

One of the good things about being an old guy is thinking back about all of the things you have done over the years. Sometimes it was my imagination, and sometimes it was real… but I did it, by golly.

I always wore my mask when I watched the Lone Ranger on TV. It was just a piece of cloth fashioned from an old rag, but it worked for me. My faithful Indian companion, Tonto, and I would ride the plains of the old west bringing peace to a lawless land. We never shot to kill. We would just shoot the pistol out of the outlaw's hands… we never spilled blood. No, siree. Dick Tracy was my favorite comic book hero. I could hardly wait for morning to check-out the Charlotte Observer's comic page to find out what happened to Dick during the overnight. I would put Dad's big hat on my little head, strap an old broken watch to my arm which served as a "two-way wrist radio," and I was ready to fight crime in the big city. No bank robber ever got away while I was on patrol.

I always sang on the Grand Ole Opry on Saturday night. We would tune in 50000-watt, clear channel WSM 650 on the radio and hear the Opry stars. Sometimes we would sit in the car and listen to the car radio if the house radio didn't come in clearly. I remember Roy Acuff and me doing duets of Wabash Cannonball and Great Speckled Bird. Sometimes Bill Monroe would invite me on stage to sing the high part of Blue Moon of Kentucky.

I remember the Sunday School Bible stories. I was the young lad who killed the giant, Goliath, with a slingshot. I was also the one who built the ark and saved my entire family and all of the animals from the flood. I'll never forget when the Lord parted the Red Sea for all of us Israelites so we could get to the other side safely

Just yesterday, Gaye and I went to the mountains and took a train ride to enjoy the beauty of the changing season. They told us that we could ride in any rail car that we so desired. We decided to ride in an open car. After all, when the bad guys came to rob the gold shipment or to kidnap someone on the train, I would be able to get a better shot from an open car. That lever action Winchester 44–40 saved many a' gold shipment or damsel in distress. No outlaws showed up yesterday. I imagine they heard that I was ridin' shotgun.

I was there raising the flag at Iwo Jima and I fought in Germany with Patton's 3rd Army. I was on stage with Elvis and the Beatles when they were on the Ed Sullivan Show. I would often assist the "pie throwers" or "plate spinners" on the Steve Allen Show. I was the first man to walk on the moon… you get the picture, I believe.

All it takes is a little imagination. Dream on, everybody… and Dream big. bob

CLOTHES MAKE THE MAN

People sure are funny. If you know me, you know that I do whatever I want to and really don't care what the world thinks about it. I've always been like that.

Last year I heard someone on TV say that he wears overalls all the time because they are the most comfortable things he has ever worn. I decided to get a pair. I love them and wear them anytime and anywhere I so desire. I now have five or six pair.

The thing that I find interesting and funny is all the comments I get from complete strangers… all positive I must say. Most of the comments come from young people in their 20's or 30's. The guys will say, "Man, I love your bibs." The girls will say, "You look cute in your bibs." If I had known that overalls made you look cute, I would have started wearing them years ago. It is amazing that it takes a pair of overalls to get such comments. If so many people like them, I wonder why everyone isn't wearing them? You see more girls wearing them than men… there is something sexy about that. Just my opinion.

"Clothes make the man" is a saying that I have always heard. I hope that it is not true, but it probably is. bob

BE THANKFUL

Thanksgiving, it is a time for… well, giving thanks… Most of us have a lot of things for which to be thankful.

I hope you do not become complacent and take any of your blessings for granted. Most people think of "stuff" or money or other assets when giving thanks. I appreciate all those things and feel blessed, but the most important and valuable things can't be purchased.

This morning I went to Propst to pay my farm gas bill. Another couple entered the store at the same time and they were arguing about money. She gave the clerk $.61 for gas and said, "I hope I will be able to get to work." That would not pay for a quart of gas. I told the clerk to make it $5.61. I remembered all the things that people have been giving me because I look homeless and pitiful. She did not say thank you or respond at all. Out the door she went. It didn't matter to me if she thanked me or not, but it did give me an inner empty feeling of sadness for her. Of course, she was empty (and not just in gas) and sad as well. She had no idea about all the things she has to be thankful for.

Here are a few things I am thankful for:

(1) I am thankful that my son lives close by. Forty-five miles is a lot better than six-thousand miles.

(2) I am thankful for the time that I got to spend with all of the family and friends that passed away this year.

(3) I am thankful for the 80+ year old man and teenage girl who found the Lord and got baptized recently.

(4) I am thankful for Gaye. She must truly love me because she does all she can to make sure that I am spoiled. When I got up this morning and walked into the kitchen, she was making waffles that she had planned on serving me in bed. She does things like that all the time.

(5) I am thankful for my friends. They are probably the most important thing that I have. You do not realize how good it makes me feel to know that we are here to lean on one another when necessary.

(6) I am thankful for that unthankful girl in the store today. Hopefully, she will realize that she has many blessings.

(7) I am thankful that with all my faults and with all the crazy things that I do, I am a Christian, saved by grace and NOT good works.

(8) I am very thankful for our Vets and that I was blessed to get to be one.

There are a lot of other things, but this has gone on long enough. What are you thankful for? Write them down. You will realize how rich you truly are. bob

ARE YOU SURE YOU SAW THAT?

Sometimes things are not as they appear. Several years ago, a friend of mine was mowing his lawn on a very hot summer day. He was mowing with a walk-behind lawn mower and was sweating profusely. His wife came out with a refreshing glass of ice water and told him to sit under the shade tree, drink his water, and rest for a few minutes. While he was sitting under the shade tree drinking his ice water his wife decided to mow while he rested. As he was sitting under the shade tree drinking ice water and his wife was mowing, one of his friends just happened to be riding by. His friend slowed down to make sure that my friend saw him. Fred Thompson took quite a ribbing about that. No, it was not what it appeared to be.

This morning Gaye asked me to stop at Walmart in Taylorsville and get two kinds of cheese, a gallon of milk, and some bananas on my way home from the Y. As I was walking through the parking lot to enter the store, a lady asked me if I could help her. It seems that someone had parked one of those electric shopping carts right beside of her car door and she couldn't enter her car. She wanted to know if I could move it for her. They are easy to drive, and I got it out of her way and was riding it into the store to park it where it belonged. Lo and behold, I saw two people coming out of the store that I knew. I could tell that they recognized me, but they were too far away to talk to them. Both are gossipers and both love to be the first to spread bad news. I don't know why some people feel that need. Anyway, if you hear anything about me riding a shopping cart... ignore it. bob

PATENT MEDICINES

My goodness, we have a medicine cabinet filled with all kinds of medicines... aspirin, ibuprofen, Tylenol, Excedrin, Alka Seltzer, Pepto Bismol, Mylanta, three or four kinds of eye drops, Red Oil, and the list goes on and on and on.

Things sure have changed. When I was a kid our medicine cabinet just had a few items.

We had Pepto Bismol, aspirin, Murine eye drops, merthiolate, Vicks VapoRub, and Alka Seltzer. That was about it... oh, I forgot, mineral oil.

Pepto Bismol was for upset stomach. I liked Pepto Bismol and would often drink it out of the bottle when Mama wasn't around. You see, we didn't have any soda pop around our house and that was the sweetest thing we had. We did have Kool Aid in the summer.

Murine was also a favorite of mine. The Burgess boys and I would put it in each other's eyes all the time. I don't know why we liked to do that, but we did. We liked the bottle that it came in with the glass tube that went down into the bottle with the rubber bulb on top.

We hated merthiolate. It was a red liquid that burned like fire when you would put it on a cut or scratch. If we didn't cry from the cut or scratch, we usually did when the merthiolate was applied. Mama would always blow on it after she applied it.

Alka Seltzer was a general cure-all. We took it when we just didn't feel well. It was a favorite of mine as well. It had bubbles in in that reminded me of a Coca Cola so I drank a lot of them. I'll never forget the mess I made when I put a spoonful of Kool Aid, a spoonful of sugar, and an Alka Seltzer in a glass of water at the same time. I thought the bubbles from the Alka Seltzer would make it taste like a Nehi Grape. That thing foamed over the side of the glass and it put me in the mind of Old Faithful going off.

My absolute favorite was Vicks VapoRub. Mama used that on us when we had a cold. She would rub some on our throat, chest, and put a little in our nose and we would usually be better by morning. My favorite thing about using Vicks VapoRub was the taste. After Mama applied it to the places mentioned above, she would say, "Stick your finger in the jar and get a fingerful and eat it." I loved the taste of it. When I learned to read, I read the directions and it said "NOT TO BE TAKEN INTERNALLY." Mama said not to pay any attention to that. Of course, she knew more about it than the manufacturer. Mama knows best.

I always wanted some of those Luden's Wild Cherry Cough Drops. Daddy said those things were just candy and would not let me have any. Instead, I got Smith Brothers Cough Drops. They were black and had codeine in them. They would sure stop a cough, but they didn't taste very well.

Mineral Oil was only used when I drank too much Pepto Bismol. You see, if you drank enough Pepto Bismol (and I did), it would make you irregular. Mineral Oil would make you regular. Enough about that.

We didn't really need much medicine in those days. We were all healthy. I only remember one overweight guy in my class and one or two overweight girls. We rarely went to the doctor. In the summer we played outside all day long, running, jumping, climbing trees, riding bicycles, and generally carrying on. We certainly didn't have cell phones, computers, and the things that the kids have today. All of our meals had the foods from the food groups that were recommended in those days. We didn't have bowls full of candy and a refrigerator full of soda pops like we all do today. Fast food was unheard of around here.

I think our society has regressed in many ways. We all enjoy the conveniences we have today, but they sometimes are not beneficial in the long run. I love the way we live today, but sometimes I long for the good old days. bob

NEW YEAR'S RESOLUTIONS

I have been in the market for a new herd bull for the last month or two. One of my old friends that I haven't seen in a long time had a bull that met all of my criteria. Actually, my only criteria is that it be an angus bull that throws small calves that grow like weeds.

He and I were talking about old times and the fun we used to have years ago. He asked how Billy Little is doing. I was sorry to inform him that Billy died a couple of years ago. He then asked about Carl Rector. Same thing, Carl passed not too long ago.

You know… I got to thinking on the way home. I thought of so many of my old friends that I have lost touch with. I don't know how it happened. Just went in different directions, I guess. It is a shame to allow that to happen and I'm gonna do something about it.

I don't usually make New Year's Resolutions, but I am going to this year. I resolve to renew old friendships and try to be a better friend to my current friends. bob

LIVE IN THE DAY

When I got my haircut this morning my hairdresser, <u>Crystal Barnes Pearson</u>, asked me what I have been up to. I told her, "Nothing, in particular, just the routine everyday things." I asked her, and she said the same as me, "Nothing in particular, just the routine everyday things." I think that is true for most of us.

I got to thinking about it on the way home. We do not have that many "big" days in our lives. Big things like our wedding, birthdays, first new house, and birth of our children just don't come along every day.

That's why it is important to live in the day, not tomorrow or yesterday. Yesterday is gone, and tomorrow will take care of itself. Get rid of the hate, jealousy, greed, and mean spirit that sometimes dwells in us.

This world needs a bright light… and I believe it is you. bob

EVIL IS UGLY, VIRTUE IS BEAUTIFUL

When do you find bad behavior beautiful? Never. When is an angry person pleasing to watch? Never. When does gloom and doom make you feel better? Never. When does prejudice make you feel proud? Never. When does immoral behavior make you feel clean and good? Never. When does gossip and hating someone make you feel better? Never. Again, evil is ugly.

How beautiful is it to see friends forgive one another and put their friendship back together? Very beautiful. How wonderful does it make you feel when someone displays integrity and honesty when it costs them to do so? Very wonderful. How encouraged does it make you feel when you see someone doing good when they think no one is watching? Very encouraging. Again, virtue is beautiful.

Yes, Sir, evil is ugly and Virtue is beautiful. Let's all try to practice virtue.

I rendered this from my Bible study this morning. Regardless of your belief, or lack thereof, the world will be a better place if we practice virtue. Let's all start today and see what happens. bob

A LESSON LEARNED

A couple of months ago, I was sitting in the waiting room of a tire store reading a daily motivational/devotional book called, "The Word for You Today." There was just something special about that book that I liked much better than most books of that kind. It was a year old and said "free" on it so I took it home with me.

A friend of mine named Elaine works in the store. I asked her where it came from. She said she thought a fellow named Craig put it in there. Coincidentally, I knew Craig and asked him about it. He said that he didn't put it there and knew nothing about it, but would like to have one.

I decided to call the company and order an up-to-date copy for myself and a copy for Craig... They were expensive and you had to order a minimum number of copies so I decided not to order any.

A few weeks later I saw Craig again. He asked if I had ordered our books. I told him I decided not to order. "Why?" he asked. "Too expensive," I replied. He countered my excuse and said, "You and I both know you have the money, and there is no reason you shouldn't order them. If it helps one person, it is worth it." He absolutely SHAMED me and I ordered them.

To end this shameful story, I have had so much positive feedback from the eighty-five or ninety people to whom I have given a copy of the book that it is unbelievable... and Craig is right. There was no reason whatsoever for me not to order the book.

Moral of the story. We often "know the cost of something, but not the value." Does that make sense to you? I hope so because that is the best way I can describe it. I continue to learn from life at this old age and I hope you do too. bob

A GOOD FEELING

Like all of you, I like to feel loved. I think that is a natural feeling.

I like to see love being demonstrated... especially when someone shows love to a stranger. It should be a natural response from all of us, but sometimes, pride, envy, greed, and arrogance get in the way.

One of the greatest outpourings of love that I have ever seen was when my neighbor "L", a tenant farmer, died a couple of years ago. The family did not even have the money to pay for a cheap funeral. I mentioned it on FB and the first thing I knew, people were sending me money from all over the country to help that family. We were able to pay off their grocery store bill, pay for the funeral, and give the family some spending money. I don't remember exactly, but I think we raised about $3000. Additionally, some donated food and household supplies. I will never forget that. The wonderful part of the whole story was I didn't ask for money...people just started sending it.

Yesterday I invited everyone to come to a BBQ fundraiser for a friend of mine named Renee to help with her medical bills. Today I got a message from someone from out of state who wants to send money to help her. I'm not ashamed to admit that it brought a tear to my eye.

Let's all practice love and get rid of that pride, envy, greed, and arrogance. My best to you all. bob

SLOW DOWN

I spend about an hour in my shop every morning with Bible study, playing music, and other positive reading. Sometimes I come across something that I just have to share with you. Today is one of those days.

The Taj Mahal is one of the most beautiful and costly tombs ever constructed. When the favorite wife of an Indian ruler died, he literally placed her casket in the middle of a field and started building the Taj Mahal around it. After a couple of years, he quit mourning his wife's death and his passion for the "building" increased. One day he was walking around inspecting the construction and found an old wooden box in the way. He moved it outside of the Taj Mahal and placed it in a pile of construction rubbish. It wasn't until a couple months later that he realized it was his wife's casket. The original purpose of the memorial got lost in the details of the construction.

There is a lesson here that I call "misplaced values." If you are a father/mother, your family appreciates the things you work to provide. Do you know what they really want… your time, your attention, your affection, and YOU!

J. Paul Getty, one of the richest men in the world, was a failure. Yes, I said that and it is not a misprint. He said the only envy he ever felt toward anyone was toward those people who were able to make a marriage work and live happily. "It's an art I have never been able to master," he said.

So, as you are building your Taj Mahal, try to remember your purpose for it. bob

MY FIRST CAR

I remember my first car. It was a blue 1961 Volkswagen. I bought it in 1964, my senior year in high school for $1300. I had saved $500 for a down payment from my part time job at the Winn-Dixie and borrowed $800. The payments were $60 a month, which I paid from the $88 I earned a month from my job. That didn't leave much spending money, but I got by somehow. Times have changed, haven't they?

My friend, Ned, wanted to go to Daytona Beach for Spring Break. Ned's family had moved to Daytona Beach a few years prior to this and had moved back to NC for some reason. Ned knew all about the college girls and the "goings on" and he had me convinced that we were going to have a ball… and we did.

We lit out at about 7PM on the Thursday before Easter and planned to come back on Easter Monday… two crazy, wild-eyed high school boys. We were cruising down 321, smoking cigars, and feeling like we were on top of the world. When we got to the outskirts of Columbia, SC, the engine started knocking, and the car began filling up with smoke. We stayed in a motel for the night and planned to fix the car the following morning and head on down to Daytona.

We called the VW dealership and they sent a wrecker to tow it in… No one could believe their eyes when we opened the engine compartment of that thing. There was a hole in the top of the engine where a piston had come through. I needed a new engine.

The service manager told me it would cost about $300 to replace the engine, I asked Ned how much money he had. I don't remember exactly, but it was less than $100. I had about the same amount. Things were not looking good to say the least. I called Mama and she said she would wire me the $300.

The money arrived at about the same time they completed the engine installation. The bill was about $320… slightly more than the $300 I was expecting. I had to pay the extra $20 leaving me even less money for gas, food and other things. We got to Daytona about midnight and went to sleep on the beach.

We were awakened by a policeman at about 2AM and he said it was illegal to sleep on the beach and we had to move on. Ned said he knew some people we could stay with. I do not remember If we ever found them or where we slept on that adventure.

We started home on Monday morning and I dreaded getting home. I just knew Daddy was going to "tear me up like a new ground," his favorite saying. When I walked in the door of the house that night, he just said, "Glad you made it home safely." Not a word was ever said about the $300.

This is not a very interesting story, but I think about it every Easter. Hopefully, some young person will read this and get a glimpse of the old days… or maybe some older person will recall those days and have some good memories. I can't imagine going to Daytona for 3 days with less than $100. I can't imagine our parents letting us do it… but it was a kinder and gentler time in our nation's history. The late 50's and early 60's were the best. This was my most memorable Easter. bob

A SOUR PUSS

We have all heard the saying, "you can't judge a book by the cover." It is often true, but it is just as likely to be false.

I stopped at Food Lion this morning to buy some fresh salmon steaks and was waiting in the check-out line. The man in front of me had an ingrained look on his face of a miserable person.

The cashier was counting his change, when suddenly he blurted out, "I have a $3 coupon for ice cream," as he handed it to her. Since the transaction was already complete, she had to do some paper work in order to give him his $3.

While she was doing the paperwork, he again blurted out, "All you have to do is give me $3." She explained that the paperwork had to be done first and she was going to have to get approval from a manager. When it was all done and over, he left the building looking even worse than he did before all of this happened.

The cashier checked out my one item and I was quickly out the door. As I was approaching my truck, he was pushing his cart back to the cart storage area. He stated, "That girl was so dumb she didn't even know how to give me $3." I replied, "Sir, that was your fault, not hers." He said, "You can go to hell too."

Yep, that was one case where you could judge a book by the cover.

Now, don't any of y'all act like that, encourage people and make them feel good. bob

MY FAVORITE BIRTHDAY

I have had a lot of good birthdays and here is my favorite........

Several years ago, my phone rang early one morning and it was Linda, an employee of Diane' s Dairy Center. She reminded me that it was "chicken pie day in the valley so come on by and eat with us"... "OK, I'll be there," I replied. I thought it was strange that she would call about that, but let's face it... strange things happen to me.

When I was about through with my meal, Diane came out of the kitchen and sat and talked with me for a few minutes. When she got ready to go back to the kitchen, she picked up my tab from the table and said, "Don't leave." A couple minutes later the employees came out of the kitchen with a beautiful and tasty birthday cake decorated like an American Flag. I ate a piece, shared some with those sitting around me, and took the remainder home.

That meant so much to me. All of the employees at Diane's are so good to me to this day. Of course, they are good to everyone. They always make me feel like I am somebody. No one but me knows how good that felt.

Linda, the employee who called me, shares a birthday with me. Bob

BE YOURSELF

Here is what I gleaned from my Bible Study today. Many of us can be helped by this. It is rare that I share things like this, but I believe it will be worthwhile. If I step on your toes, you will get over it, I hope. I value your friendship.

We all try to keep up with fads, styles, and the Jones' sometimes. If beards are in style, many men will grow beards. If a certain hair color is in style, many women make a beeline to the salon. Sometimes it is popular to have a tan, sometimes it is popular to be pale. Sometimes we want long hair or sometimes we want short hair depending on what everyone else is doing. If your neighbor buys an acre of land, you go somewhere and buy two acres. Sometimes we buy a new car because our neighbor or friend got a new one… I believe you get the picture.

We devote our energies to meeting the latest "standard." That "standard" will soon change and you have to start anew. We all do it and it is an endless pursuit.

Don't become so involved into fitting into this culture that you act without even thinking. You will not find beauty and peace by comparing yourself to athletes, movie stars, etc. That image is unsustainable. You will find peace by asking God to remove the scales from your eyes and show you what you look like in His eyes.

Psalm 3 says, "Those who look to Him are radiant." Be a God pleaser, not a people pleaser. bob

THE SCARY RODEO

This story takes place on Halloween night about twenty or twenty-five years ago.

I had gone to Greensboro, NC to judge a rodeo. It was a cool night, the bulls were bucking well, and the cowboys were riding well. It was just a perfect night for a rodeo…

The rodeo ended. I went to the concession stand and got a soda pop and a couple of hot dogs to eat on the long ride back home in my 90 something Ford pickup with a camper cover on the bed.

I collected my pay and pulled out of the parking lot. I checked my rearview mirror, and in the mirror, I saw a slender head, with a scruffy goatee staring at me with a look of total horror on his face from inside the camper cover. Knowing that the young bull riders would go to any length to play a trick or joke on me, I thought it was a Halloween mask and I wondered how they did that. When I got in a certain light, the face would reflect into the windshield. It was spooky and a good trick.

After a few seconds, the skinny head of a young lady appeared. I thought, "This is amazing, I can't wait to get back home and see how they did this." Then I heard someone beating on the window and yelling, "Stop, stop!" My Lord, there was actually a real live person back there. I pulled over and it was a young boy and girl of about 17 or 18 years old trying to find a warm place to be together. They "freshened up," got in the cab of the truck with me where it was warm, and I took them back to the rodeo parking lot. Those two young'uns were just shaking and shivering like a leaf. I do not know if it was because they were cold or because they were scared to death. Bob

LEGACY?

About twenty years ago, I worked with a fellow who had just been dismissed from the place that we worked. I'm not sure if he was fired, downsized, or resigned. That was a long time ago.

The week after his employment ended, he called me and asked me to meet him for lunch. While we were eating he asked, "What do you think my legacy will be?" I was taken back by the question and was pretty much at a loss for words. A legacy is something we leave behind. It could be assets like money, property, or it could be an achievement.

I answered his question simply by saying that, "I didn't know." He was very much concerned about his legacy and would not let it go. I finally told him that very few people leave a legacy. A legacy is usually left by people like George Washington, Davy Crocket, or Elvis Presley. I also explained to him that a legacy could be good or bad.

Instead of worrying about our legacy, let us think about how we can IMPACT people now in a positive way.

Many years ago, I worked at the Winn-Dixie when I was in high school. One Saturday afternoon a stranger came into the store and bought a big buggy full of groceries. After I bagged them, he told me that he was the new pastor of the church across the road and, "Would I take his groceries to the parsonage adjacent to the church?" I put his groceries on the kitchen table and he picked up a basket of white seedless grapes that he had purchased and said, "Eat some of these, they will be refreshing to you." That has been over 50 years ago and I still remember it. You see, he impacted my life just by being kind and thoughtful.

About 10 years ago, I was mowing my sister's lawn in South Newton and this same man was walking by. I jumped off the lawnmower and ran out to the street to chat with him. He told me that he was walking to town to mail his wife a birthday card. I didn't understand. "Why not just hand it to her?" He said it means "so much more to someone if they get a card in the mail."

From that time on, I started mailing Gaye's anniversary and birthday cards. Yes, it does make a difference. Just recently this same man told me to spend some time writing letters and cards instead of texting or emailing. He said that it is good for both parties. You see, he impacted my life again. That is a legacy. bob

TRAIN RIDES AND POOL ROOMS

Train rides are usually part of our vacations every year. Gaye and I have ridden just about every steam engine and antique train east of the Mississippi. So far, we haven't ridden a train this year. Here is the reason I have such a fascination with trains:

Our family did most of our shopping in Newton NC, my hometown, when I was a lad. We didn't have a car during those early years and Newton was within easy walking distance from our home. Every Friday when Daddy got paid, we would walk to town for groceries and other necessities to last us for the week. That is the way it was for many of the WWII veterans just starting out in life with a family...

About once a month, we would walk to North Newton on Saturday morning and board the train to Hickory, a distance of about 10 miles, for a little shopping at Sears Roebuck and Company. Mama and Daddy both liked to go to Sears Roebuck and look around at all the wonderful things under one roof. When we got to Sears, we would split up. Daddy and I would go to the hardware section and sporting goods. Mama and my sister, Patsy, would look at dresses, perfumes, jewelry... you know, lady's things. We rarely bought anything... just dreamed.

When we got through at Sears, we would go in different directions to explore the stores and wonders of the "Big City." Mama would always say, "Earl, don't you take Bobby to that pool room."

As soon as Mama and Patsy got out of sight, Daddy and I would walk across the street to the pool room.

I never did understand why Mama didn't want me to go in there… probably because there was a little gambling and drinking going on… and an occasional fight would break out. My favorite part was eating the hot dogs for 15 cents. Daddy and I would eat two each and drink a 6 oz Coca Cola from a bottle. I can still smell the wonderful aroma of that pool room and the taste of those hot dogs was exquisite. Mama never did know about that. We always told her that we ate at Woolworth's lunch counter. I think a little white lie is ok every now and then, especially if no one is hurt by it.

At 2 o'clock we would rejoin Mama and Patsy at Sears where we would each get a nickel bag of candy to eat on the return trip home. That was so much fun.

I still like pool rooms and trains. It is hard to find a "real, authentic pool room" anymore. If there was one around here, I feel certain I would go often. The last one closed 10 or 15 years ago.

Well, the trains are still around. I didn't think we were going to get a train ride this year until Gaye informed me that she made reservations on one of the steam engines that winds around the North Carolina mountains every Fall. That is my favorite way to see the Fall foliage.

This has been a favorite childhood memory of mine. bob

OLD SCHOOL

Some of my fondest memories of growing up in Newton, center around the old Newton Elementary School on North Ashe Avenue. I attended there my first six years of school from 1952 through 1958.

I don't know how it is now, but in those days, we had "play period" every day. Sometimes it was a structured time when we would choose up sides and play softball, dodge ball or volleyball, and sometimes the teacher would just "turn us loose" and tell us to be back to the room in 30 minutes.

On the days when we were turned loose most of us would go to the playground… and a playground it was. It had two sliding boards, one large and one small. We would always take a piece of wax paper to school with us to sit on when we were sliding. It would make you go a lot faster.

The monkey bars were always a favorite. We had two sets of them as well, one large and one small. We would climb all over those things and hang by our legs and do all kinds of crazy stunts. It was always fun.

We also had a seesaw and tether ball. I rarely did those. The seesaw was never something that I enjoyed. and the 8th graders usually took over the tether ball.

My favorite was the swings. We had two large sets of swings and one small swing. I would always take off running for the big swings and would swing for the entire 30 minutes. You could really go high on those things. I remember that if you STOOD UP on the swings you could see the tip top of the flagpole which was on the opposite side of the two-story school. We would swing so high that we would be horizontal at the peak of the swing.

It could never be like that again… probably because of liability issues. I do remember a boy falling off the monkey bars and breaking his arm. I am sure his parents never even thought about a lawsuit because he was unattended. Things are different now, and as far as I know schools no longer have that type of playground equipment, and certainly you would be supervised if they did…

I am a "senior citizen" now and the old school is long gone. That was a long time ago. I often think of those days when I ride down a residential street and do not see any kids playing outside. They are probably inside on the computer because it is too dangerous to play outside unsupervised these days… sadly, they are missing a lot… bob

THE WEDDING RING

When Gaye put that wedding ring on my finger, June 20, 1970, I vowed to myself that I would never take it off under any circumstances.

A couple of years later, I looked at my hand and the ring was gone. I had no idea where I had lost it and I sure didn't want to tell Gaye that it was gone. After all, her favorite song at the time was the Charlie Pride classic, "Does my ring hurt your finger when you go out at night?" I didn't want to arouse any suspicions or make her feel hurt in any way.

What to do? I decided to go to the Jewelry Store where she purchased the ring, and buy one just like it, and even have the inside of the ring engraved the same way. That's what I did. My plan worked well and she didn't know the difference.

We were eating supper about a month later, and Gaye asked, "Have you lost anything?" "No", I replied, having forgotten about the ring. She held up the original ring and said, "Look what I found… I picked up an old pair of work gloves this afternoon and felt something in the finger and it was your ring." She then asked for my hand so she could put it back on my finger. I sat on my left hand and told her we could do it later. Talk about an awkward moment. She insisted on doing it then and I had to "fess up." I took the new ring off my finger and she put the old one back on my finger. I liked that. It was kind of like renewing your vows. I am still wearing that ring and have never removed it. Luckily for me, she is a good-hearted woman (in love with a good-timing man) and she just laughed.

I am one lucky (and spoiled) man. She understands me and loves and accepts me for what I am, whatever that is. bob

FUNERALS

On a November evening in 1992, I was listening to radio station WSM AM 650 Nashville, Tennessee. The DJ announced that the King of Country Music, Roy Acuff, had died from congestive heart failure in a Nashville hospital. The next morning when I woke up, I turned the radio on the same station and they announced that Mr. Acuff had been buried during the night. His request was to be buried as soon as possible with no fanfare. His family followed his wish to the T. I think about that often for some reason.

I remember when my Grandmother Marlowe died in 1955, my Dad spent the night in the funeral home with her the night before she was buried. That was called "sitting up with the dead." I do not know the reason for that… probably just a way of showing respect.

About twenty years ago, a millionaire friend of mine died. His wife put him in, what she said was a $500 pine box casket. He told her not to waste money on an expensive casket. He was always practical AND cheap until the end.

On the other end of the spectrum, I know a family that is probably lower middle class (or maybe upper-end poor) who are making payments on a $15,000 funeral. She wanted to put him away in style.

When Mom died, she told me that she just wanted a grave side service with her casket closed. She said she didn't want people walking by there looking at her. That's what I did. I guess there is no wrong way to have a funeral. I have no idea where I am going with it. Nowhere, I guess. I just felt like writing about Mr. Acuff, a hero of mine. As a classic country music historian, I suppose I just wanted to keep Mr. Acuff's legacy alive. Graves are too deep of a subject for a simple-minded thing like me to write about anyway. bob

ME AND MY BIG MOUTH

Well, I have done it again. That big #13 that I wear fits perfectly in my mouth sometimes.

Gaye and I stopped at Walmart to get a few things today. We were standing in the checkout line waiting our turn. The lady in front of me was emptying her basket. She was having trouble getting a large turkey out of the buggy, so naturally, I assisted her.

She said, "Has anyone ever told you that you look like Andy Griffith?" "No", I replied, "I have never heard that before." She responded, "Can you guess the name of the famous person that I look like?" Without hesitation, I immediately replied, "Ray Price, the country singer who passed away a couple of years ago." With a distant, faraway look on her face she said, "Barbara Bel Geddes, the mother on Dallas, is who most people say." I told her that I always thought that Ray Price and Barbara Bel Geddes looked alike.

Sometimes Gaye has to act like she doesn't know me. bob

FEAR

FEAR. We all have FEARS. Some of us are AFRAID of heights, some are AFRAID of public speaking, and others are AFRAID of snakes, etc. These are all natural, innate FEARS that we all have to some extent or the other.

I heard on the radio that a certain radio station would not play Frosty the Snowman. They said that Frosty has "two eyes made out of coal" and the mere mention of the word "coal" would SCARE people. After all, when Frosty melts, the coal will be left on the ground to pollute the earth.

I also heard that some college students saw a Confederate Flag on a car near their campus. They reported this sighting to the college administration. They said the sight of the flag SCARED them and they were AFRAID. They were provided counseling because of this incident.

First of all, let me say that I do not want to hear your opinion on the Confederate Flag or coal. I have heard all those arguments and that is not what this post is about.

I want to know how people have developed FEARS of things like flags or two pieces of coal? Those have to be learned FEARS....not innate or natural FEARS that I mentioned in the first paragraph.

In FDR's Inaugural Speech, he said, "The only thing we have to FEAR is FEAR itself." I believe those words to be true. The thing that I am most concerned about is why people seem to be substituting FEAR for sound reasoning these days.

Please, my friends, don't go through life being AFRAID. Learn to face your FEARS and whip them. I know that is hard to do, but give it a try. bob

OUR FIRST TELEVISION

I remember the first TV that Gaye and I ever had. This is a funny story about the first day we had the TV. It was a 19" table model, color TV. I bought it, and the antenna on a Saturday afternoon in 1971. I couldn't wait to get home and install it.

The antenna kit that I bought was the kind you use to mount the antenna on a pole attached to the side of the house. When I was mounting the pole to the side of the house, the bracket was missing that held the pole to the side of the house. What to do? I decided to staple a wire on each side of the pole which would probably be ok until I could get a proper bracket.

In those days you had to buy an electronic device called a "Tenna Rotor." A Tenna Rotor would turn the antenna toward the station you were watching to insure good reception. It included a motor that mounted to the antenna and a device in the house that sat on top of the TV which would activate the antenna to turn toward the station you were watching.

I finally got my antenna and Tenna Rotor hooked up, and went into the house to watch my very own TV for the first time. We could watch 3 stations in Charlotte and 1 in Hickory. Occasionally we could get other stations if the weather was right.

Everything worked perfectly… at first. The longer I watched the TV, and the more I switched stations, the worse the reception became. I had no idea what was going on.

At that time, we were living in a housing development with neighbors beside and behind us. The phone rang and it was our backyard neighbor, Ray. Ray said, "Bob, I don't know what is going on, but there is a TV antenna rolling around in your back yard." In those days all of the guys in the neighborhood would get together on Saturday afternoon and we would have a drink or two or three together. I think Ray must have thought he had one too many and was seeing things.

Anyway, here is what happened. The temporary wire that I used to attach the antenna pole to the house broke loose. The antenna, the pole, and the Tenna Rotor motor fell to the ground. Every time I would try to change the direction of the antenna from inside the house, it would cause the antenna to roll around in the yard. (That was hard to explain, but some of you, older people will understand.) That was one of the funniest things I had ever seen. bob

RESPECT

While watching a bit of American Idol tonight, a young fellow said "Yes, Sir" to the guy who sends them onto the stage to perform. The guy said, "Don't say yes, sir, …say yeah, bro."

A little later in the show, someone said "Yes, sir" to the guy who was screening them. He said to the kid, "Don't say yes, sir… I don't like that."

I have a lot of young friends. Some call me Mr. Bob, some say Bob, some say Mr. Marlowe, and others say Sir. All of them have been taught to show respect. I haven't necessarily earned any respect, but they are taught to be respectful. I would never tell them not to show respect to their elders as they have been taught.

I guess I am old school. bob

WIND CHILL FACTOR

This will probably be too much information for some of you. If you get your feelings hurt easily, are easily embarrassed, or are politically correct, or can conjure up a vivid picture in your mind, please stop reading NOW and move on to something else.

A man came by the house this morning to check something about the electricity before they hookup the new power line to our new circuit breaker and meter box. He had to turn the electricity off.

At about that same time I had to use the bathroom. I wouldn't be able to use an inside bathroom because the well water pump would not work without electricity. I would have only been able to flush once and if that "low water usage" commode of ours didn't get the job done with one flush, I would be out of luck.

I decided to go out and squat behind the barn. It was 35 degrees and the wind was blowing… I have no idea what the wind chill factor was. (We need to do away with the wind chill factor anyway. I never got nearly as cold as I do now before they invented it, but that is another post for another time.)

I now fully understand what that well digger and brass monkey were talking about. bob

OLD DOGS AND WATERMELON WINE

There ain't nothin' in this old world worth a solitary dime 'cept old dogs and children and watermelon wine." That is a line from a Tom T. Hall song that I always enjoyed.

Never have had any watermelon wine to be honest with you. I 'spect I would probably like it. If I ever get to drink some of it, I hope it is made out of the old-timey watermelons instead of those new-fangled ones that do not have seeds. I never have had one of those that tastes like a real watermelon. Besides, I like to spit the seeds. I'm going to go online today and order some watermelon seeds that produce old-timey watermelons and make some watermelon wine this summer. I plan to leave the seeds in the wine. Hopefully, my sophisticated guests won't mind spitting the seeds as they drink their wine out of a Dixie cup. We'll see about that.

I know a good bit about old dogs. I have had several that died of old age. We have three dogs now, and one is about eleven and it is easy to see that he is slowing down. Kinda like me, I guess. Everyone says that when the world turns against you, your dog will still be there for you. That's the truth. When our old dog is in the house, he will put his front legs on the arm of the chair and lay his head on my chest and start purring like a kitten. I believe that he realizes that his days may be numbered and is asking me to give him the unconditional love that he has given me for all these years. I will do that. bob

OYSTER STEW

Ladies and Gentlemen, please do not take this as me being boastful, but I have developed the most perfect recipe for Oyster Stew in the world. I will be generous and share it at no cost to you. I want to add some happiness to your life today.

Ingredients:
1 slice bacon
1 slice onion (finely chopped)
1/4 stick of butter (give or take)
1 qt whole milk
1 pt (8 ounces) oysters (found in the refrigerated case)

Instructions:

Begin frying bacon at low heat in skillet. As bacon is frying, cut it into small pieces. When the bacon is about 1/2 done add the onion. Then put the butter into the same pan and let it begin melting among the bacon and onion. Then pour in the oysters (juice and all). As the oysters are cooking use a knife and cut them into small pieces. After about 5 or 6 minutes or so the oysters should be about done. Pour the entire contents of that pan (bacon, bacon drippings, onion, butter, and oysters) into a pot and add the milk. Cook it slowly, being careful not to boil the mixture, for about 15 or 20 minutes. Salt and pepper or use other seasoning to taste. It tastes better the second day.

I have worked for years to perfect this recipe and am sharing it with you free of charge. That is just the kind of guy that I am.

You're welcome. bob

OLD PEOPLE

As I looked down at the congregation from my front row balcony seat, it occurred to me that our church has a young congregation and there are no old people there. The church was full and vibrant this past Sunday, but no old people.

What happened to the old people? I remembered all the Sigmon's, Eckard's, Huffman's, and Little's. They were old people. There were several different clans of all these names, and at least 3 generations of each clan. I asked myself once again, "Where are all the old people?

I remember going to meetings at the church 40 years ago and being amazed and impressed at the wisdom of the old people. They could remember things that happened many years prior and could somehow combine those memories with their wisdom and make excellent decisions for the church.

It finally occurred to me that the old people have gradually died off, one by one. It just happened so slowly that no one, or at least me, didn't realize it was happening.

Could it be that I am now one of the old people? It was rude of me to use the term old people earlier in this writing. I apologize for that… now that I realize that I am an "old people." Yes, Sir, our church does have old people, I just didn't realize until now that I am one of them. There ain't no such thing as old people, just senior citizens.

Yep, I'm an "old people" now… I mean senior citizen. Hopefully, my generation will be able to pass on the things we learned over the years to the younger generations, just like the generation before us shared their wisdom. That's our job, you know.

What happened to the years from the time I was a youngster until the time that I became an old person… I mean senior citizen? I just don't know. Time inches along at a faster rate than you realize and suddenly you realize you ARE a senior citizen.

As I look back at some of the things that are important to me, things like graduating from high school, my military and Vietnam years, getting married, the birth of our son etc., it is hard to believe that those things happened 40 or 50 years ago. Those things seem like just yesterday. Where did the time go?

Time and age are among our greatest assets. Use them wisely. Don't look back with regrets. The road goes on forever, but the highway never ends. bob

A SENIOR MOMENT

A funny thing happened this morning at the store where I buy coffee, as I make my rounds of the farms.

There was an old lady in the store also buying a cup of coffee. As usual, I was chatting with her like I do everyone I see. She was probably not all that old… maybe even younger than me. I have trouble telling young from old people these days. Let's just say she was a "seasoned citizen," (If I use the word "seasoned citizen" one more time it is mine. My senior high school English teacher taught us that if you use a new word twice, it is yours.)

This seasoned citizen (it is mine) told me that she had hypothermia. I thought she was simply referring to the cold weather that we have been experiencing this past week and that she was having trouble staying warm. I told her that, "I have it too," She asked, "What do you do for yours?" I told her that I wear layers, a hat, and gloves when I am outside and that seems to help." I also told her that we have a fine new heating system in our house, plus a woodstove that we like to use and that we stay very warm and comfortable. (At this point, she was giving me strange looks.)

She said that her house is warm too. She then added that she had even tried drinking warm milk before bed and had started taking Tylenol PM, and she still couldn't sleep. This conversation was starting to seem very strange and weird.

When I got into the truck, it occurred to me what she was trying to tell me. She was trying to say that she had insomnia… not hypothermia… just using the wrong word. We were talking about two totally different things. That's the way we seasoned citizens are, we understand each other. bob

KEEP GROWING

Sometimes people just seem to give up on life and the excitement and joy of life slowly dwindles away. I know many people like that. That is particularly true of "seasoned citizens" like me and many of you… but it doesn't have to be like that.

Remember when you were young, I mean young, maybe five or six years old. New things were happening in our lives and we were excited about it. Things like learning to read, count, ride a bicycle, climbing trees, driving nails, or whatever you did for the first time. We had new adventures every day.

A few years later you learned to play organized sports and you started to become a little more "social," By the time you became a teenager, you were learning to drive the family car in the driveway….and just couldn't wait to get your driver's license. There was always a new challenge before us and always something to look forward to.

The next thing you knew, you were looking forward to graduating from high school and attending college, joining the military, or getting a job. There was always something new on the horizon.

When you get to be "seasoned," you often think you have done it all and there are no new adventures. That is wrong thinking. I believe that Colonel Sanders was in his 60's before he started his Kentucky Fried Chicken chain. It is never too late to learn something new, and new challenges abound if you look for them.

I have friends that can tell you about every program on TV. They schedule their life around the TV listing. Don't let that happen to you. Get out and do something productive… and there is always something you can do or some place that you will fit in and are needed. Get involved in a charity, church, or even a political campaign… just do something. Take on a new hobby or learn to play an instrument… anything to keep your mind active.

I have always wanted to learn to draw or paint pictures. I know that seems strange to those of you who know me well. That is about as foreign to me as speaking Arabic, but I believe I can learn. I have already been working on it and look forward to warm weather when I can get outside and do some landscapes, etc.

I hope that all my young AND "seasoned" friends continue to look for new challenges and to stay away from the recliner. bob

THE POWER OF PRAYER

I have a friend in Tennessee with severe back problems. The doctors have recommended that he have surgery. He is not quite sure he wants to do that. After all, we often hear stories about people who have had back surgery and ended up worse than they were. He said he was going to pray himself through this. It reminded me of a story that I remember from the 70's or 80's when I was still working.

One morning one of my salesmen came in for his visit like he did every Monday morning. After discussing business, he told me that he would not be here the next week because he was going to have a hernia repaired, and that he would be out of commission for a couple weeks.

The next Monday he called on me like he always did. When we sat down to talk, I said "your surgery must have gone really well for you to be here today." He said that he didn't have the surgery. Here is what happened:

He said he went to the hospital for his surgery and the first thing he knew, he was asleep in the Operating Room. Later when he was in the Recovery Room taking oxygen, he could hear his wife and the nurses talking, laughing, and giggling. He was too "out of it" to know what was happening…

When he finally got awake enough to know what was going on, they told him that his hernia had disappeared and there was no trace of it. Let me tell you something, friends, hernias do not JUST disappear.

He told me that he had been praying about it fervently with all his heart, and that he believed that the Lord would take care of it.... and He did. Yes, sir, I believe in the power of prayer.

Today I pray that each of us will have the faith of a child and that we all learn to turn things over to the Lord and not try to depend on ourselves. bob

THEY PUT ME IN THE MOVIE

My best bet is that you do not know that I was a movie star at one time. Yes, sir, I appeared in a movie about 10 or 15 years ago.

We got a call one night from a company wanting to work out a deal and make a movie on our farm. We were picked because our farm is on the Historic Register and they had seen a picture of it in some book or magazine and thought that it would be a perfect setting. Everything worked out and they were soon at the 100-year-old farm house and filming began.

They used the inside and outside of the house, plus our farm land and timber tracts. It amazed me how they would re-arrange things for different scenes and how they always put things back in perfect order. There were always at least 50 people coming or going all the time. This went on for probably 6 weeks.

There were a lot of highfalutin' people hanging around here. Most of them never seemed to quite understand Gaye and me or our lifestyle. They would ask all kinds of questions during down time about how and why we did things, but I don't think some of them ever fully grasped it. I will never forget toward the end of the shoot, a man from Atlanta said he would "give anything to live like we live." I think that many of them would love to get away from the high-stress lifestyles, but do not know how or are afraid to for some reason. One young girl from Baltimore would come back in the evening just to sit on the porch. I think she understood.

When I got home from church on the last day of the shoot, the producer was there. I could always tell that he liked me. His wife would give me gifts. He said, "Bob, can you load a horse into a trailer?"

"Yes Sir," I replied. He then told me that he wanted me to be in the movie, and they needed someone to load a horse in the last scene. Now I became a movie star.

You should have seen me. It probably took about 20 times until I got it right. Sometimes I would walk around the trailer too fast or too slowly, sometimes too far away from the trailer or too close, and sometimes a combination of each. It was always something, but I finally got it right. When the scene was over, I found out why they picked me for the job. It seems that the person who was supposed to have loaded the horse got kicked in the ribs by the horse and was in the Emergency Room. Then one of the stage hands (or whatever you call them} tried to load the horse and it dragged him across the pasture and into a creek. Everyone was afraid of the horse. I probably would have been also had I known what had happened to the others.

You should have seen Gaye and me at the movie premiere which was held at a theater in Charlotte. That must have been a sight. There we were, straight from Route 1, Claremont, NC... lined up in a long procession of fine Cadillacs and limousines waiting for our time to pull up to the door of the theater and be escorted to our seats. Flashbulbs flashing, adoring fans hollering and screaming was all we could see for a block. Gaye and I were smiling and waving, just as if we were somebody. I lowered the windows and they would run up to the truck to shake our hands. We didn't have on a tux or evening dress either... just regular clothes for us. In fact, we didn't rent a limousine or Cadillac either. We were in our best truck.

Somehow, I think the others were envious of us. Some people just do not know how to be themselves... I learned long ago that happiness and contentment are two things that many people do not have and don't know how to get it. I can promise you this... you will never find happiness or contentment trying to impress others and being something that you aren't.

You can take the boy out of the country, but you can't take the country out of the boy. I ain't changing. bob

THE WHEEL BARREL?

This has been a good morning so far. After giving the cows some grain and making sure they are all present and accounted for, I then went to Lowes to buy a wheelbarrow.

I walked all around Lowes and could not find a wheelbarrow anywhere. I finally asked a young employee and she said, "They are hard to find, and I will show you." We walked down an aisle and she said, "They are here somewhere, just hard to locate." A wheel barrow is fairly large and visible and I could tell there were not any there. She finally said, "here they are" and pointed to them. It was a wheel bearing. I told her I wanted a wheelbarrow, not a wheel bearing. She said, "I am not sure what a wheelbarrow is… describe it to me." After describing it to her she said, "What you want is a wheel BARREL." I got a fine one with two wheels on the front which will make balancing it easier.

On the way home, I noticed that the "HOT" light was on at Krispy Kreme. The truck kept trying to turn into the parking lot, but somehow, I evaded KK. I later rode by Dunkin Doughnuts and evaded that also. It was all I could do to stay away, but I did.

Well, I need to mow the yard so I had better go. First, I am going to stencil 'HERS' on the wheelbarrow. bob

GOOD FRIENDS

Sometimes we can let the events of the world and nation bring us down to a low point. Admittedly, I have allowed it to happen to me in recent days, but it didn't last long.

This beautiful, peaceful community has changed quite a bit in the forty years that I have lived here. Some changes for the good, some not so good. At one time this was a close-knit community of friends. We all knew each other and considered one another friends. Much of the beautiful, rolling farmland has now turned into housing developments and sub divisions. I no longer even know most of the people who live close by. I guess that is my fault.

When I turned on the radio this morning, there was the usual bad news concerning the nation and world. I have become numb to that and can handle it pretty well… then the local news came on…

There was a double homicide yesterday at a house less than a mile from me. The details are still sketchy, but it was apparently a man and wife who were killed. To make it worse, they have a 10-year old daughter, who I imagine was in school. Things like that aren't supposed to happen in Route 1, Claremont, NC. Those things are reserved for Chicago, Detroit, Charlotte, LA, and New York...or at least I thought so. What in the world is going on?

When I turned on Facebook, the first thing I read was from a good friend who lives a few miles away whose home was broken into yesterday while they were at work. I just do not understand these things.

After reading on Facebook, I went out to Bob and Gaye's Pickin' and Grillin' Parlor to eat breakfast and do my Bible Study. I started to feel revived and much better. Looking at the beauty of God's world and counting my many blessings really helped a lot.

Here is the good news:

After going to Y and feeding the cows at both places, Gaye and I went to vote. While standing in line at the polling place, I was talking to my friends Dennis and Margaret. I then heard someone behind me say, "I get to vote behind Bob Marlowe." I turned and it was two more of my friends. Dennis said, "I believe you know everyone in the county." That made me feel good and help me realize how many friends I have.

Of course, we all have "down" time, but it doesn't have to last long. Count your friends and other blessings, look around at God's beautiful creation, listen to or make music, and think about all of the people who love you and care about you. That "down" time will soon disappear.

In Matthew, Jesus said, "Look at the birds of the air, for they neither sow nor reap nor gather into barns; yet your Heavenly Father feeds them. Are you not of more value than they?" I ain't got nuthin' to worry about or fear... neither do you. I hope this helps some of you along your way. bob

BE A GOOD RECEIVER

We have had a good morning. I am getting ready to move the cows at the remote location to Spring/Summer pastures, so Gaye and I went over there to check fences this morning. We finally got the electric part of the fence working and were on the way home.

As we were driving home, I asked Gaye if she would like to stop at Papa's Restaurant beside of Lake Lookout for lunch. Papa's is not a restaurant where I often eat, but they have good country food. I ordered an open face steak sandwich and Gaye ordered a cheeseburger. We both had tea.

When we finished, I reached for my wallet to leave a tip, but it was not in my back pocket where it belonged. I know what happened. Knowing that I was going to be on my knees and crawling around while working on fences, I put on my dirty overalls, which were in the dirty clothes, and did not go back to the bedroom where my wallet was located. Gaye didn't bring her purse so it looked like we were going to get to wash dishes.

After telling the manager what happened, she told me that I could bring her the money at my convenience and not to worry about it. About that time a fellow jumped up and came running over there and said he would be honored to pay our bill. I did not know him, but I did know his wife. I offered to repay him, but he would not hear of it. In fact, I went on and on and on... about repaying him.

Here are my thoughts on this matter. (1) It is wonderful to live in this part of the world where there are so many kind people. (2) What is it that makes it so hard to just say, "Thank You"? That is all he wanted, just a thank you, but I went on and on and on. Shame on me.

Moral of the story: It is just as important to be a gracious receiver as it is a gracious giver. I need to work on that. bob

WONDERFULLY MADE

A recent report said that 75% of all doctor's visits are a result of "bad behavior" on the part of the patient. That really doesn't surprise me at all. It is certainly true in my case.

A 30-year old single woman was continually visiting her doctor. She said she didn't feel well, but test after test showed that everything was ok. The doctor told her to keep taking her medicine for depression, high blood pressure, and cholesterol, and she would be fine.

One night, in a dream, the reason for her health issues occurred to her. She realized that she no longer liked herself and what she had become. She needed to make changes......and make changes she did.

First, she started eating properly… no sugar, no between-meal snacks, no drinking her problems away......just 3 square meals a day. After a week or two, she was feeling a little better and… "hmmm, wonder what exercise will do for me????"

She started out trying to walk a mile every evening. It took its toll on her out-of-shape, overweight body, but it soon became much easier. She then decided to jog a little bit in her mile walk. Pretty soon she was up to walking and jogging two miles per evening. One night she actually ran the whole two miles.

As a career woman, working her way to the top, she was accustomed to working long hours… and she would never leave the office until after the boss had left. She changed her attitude on that and was the first one out the door at 5 o'clock. She soon found she was getting more work done than ever and was up for another promotion.

Long story short, six months later she ran a 10K. Six months after that, she ran her first marathon… 26.2 miles. She was also promoted to Executive Vice President at work. She was now feeling great and all of her health problems, both physical and mental, had disappeared… and she was off all her meds.

The Bible says that our bodies are "wonderfully made." You see, it is already in us to be what God wants us to be. It is up to us to bring it out. Let's work on that. bob

THE GUNSLINGER

A funny thing happened to me today. This morning I picked up an almost- empty bag of cow feed. A mouse jumped out of the bag and landed in my pocket. I was dancing around, shaking all over, got my overalls unhooked in record time, and shook the mouse out. It must have been a sight to see. That was another one of those Kodak moments that I often have.

Speaking of dancing, here is funny story that I remember hearing long ago:

In the days of the old west, there was a mean gunslinger who lived in town. Yes, sir, he was mean and everyone was afraid of him. One day a farmer rode into town in a wagon, pulled by a mule.

The gunslinger went up to the farmer and said, "I want to see you dance." The farmer said, "I don't know how to dance." The gunslinger pulled out both of his six shooters and started shooting at the direction of the farmers feet. Dust was flying everywhere, but the farmer did not move a step.

When the gunslinger ran out of bullets, the farmer reached into his wagon and pulled out a Winchester rifle. He aimed the rifle at the gunslinger and said, "Have you ever kissed an old mule's stinking a$$?" The gunslinger, scared for the first time, replied, "No, but I have always wanted to."

Well, at least I thought it was funny. bob

THE BRIGHT SIDE

Today has started off good. Shoot, all days are good, even when some would say that things are bad… you just have to look for the good. That is how Gaye is. She sees all things positively and never seems to worry about anything.

Gaye is getting a newly decorated bathroom this week. They will finish it today. We didn't plan it like that, but that is the way it has worked out. Here is what happened:

A couple of years ago we bought a new commode and sink. When the plumber was installing the commode, he said, "This doesn't seem to be sealed right, but I guess it is." Well, it wasn't. Long story short, every time we flushed the commode, some of the water leaked between the ceramic tile and the sub-floor and eventually caused the sub-floor to rot. It all had to be torn out and, as a result, Gaye gets a new bathroom. It looks good and we are proud it. Just think, if that plumber had installed that commode properly, we wouldn't have a newly designed bathroom. Thank God for shoddy plumbers.

Also, we are getting a new porch of the <u>Stan Hitchcock</u> design. They are going to start on it today or tomorrow. I have been repairing it for several years, but I have run out of the tongue and groove boards that it requires, and am going to replace it with just plain old deck boards.

Sometimes it is good when things go wrong. It opens the door for new opportunities. bob

THE BARLOW KNIFE

It's just an old, cheap, Barlow knife. Paint worn off, rusty blades... but it still is still functional. This knife has been in battle all over Europe and North Africa in WW11 during the early 40's... It has also traveled the rivers of the Mekong Delta in Vietnam from 1967 to 1969. This knife has endured a lot....and, again, it is functional.

Dad gave it to me when I was in the first grade. Although it has very little monetary value, this knife is very valuable to me. You see, it has a story to tell......if only it could talk.

Some of us are getting rusty, and our paint is worn thin, but we must endure.... just like that knife, we must tell our story.

When I was a kid and was sad about some little old thing, Dad would say, "Who licked the red off your candy?" We still sometimes get "the red licked off our candy," don't we? I know that I do.

Sometimes I believe that it is God talking to us when we get the "red licked off our candy." He is trying to get our attention, and is telling us to listen to Him, pray, and get back in the Word. He will give you a brand-new red sucker and sharpen your blades… if you will just listen. bob

FARMING

In most businesses, you can usually succeed if you work hard, spend wisely, and keep abreast of business conditions and trends. Not true in all instances, especially farming. The farmer buys fertilizer, seed, expensive equipment, and works long hours only to be held hostage by weather conditions and market prices. Although we are not officially in a drought situation, it sure looks and feels as if we are… things are very dry in this part of North Carolina. The hayfields are only about six inches high and the grass is already heading out. It should be knee high by now. That is a big concern for a lot of people. It doesn't look like there will be a Spring cutting of hay… or at least not much of one.

We can't control the weather. A couple of months ago I spent $4000 for lime and fertilizer, and that was for just part of the farms. I would have been better off to go to Vegas and play the slots. The lime and fertilizer just didn't pay off… not at all.

Luckily for me, the cattle business is not something that I depend on for my livelihood. It is just something that I HAVE to do. It is not in me to just quit. It is a lifestyle that I enjoy… it is an addiction and is as hard to quit as any drug.

Last week at one of the livestock markets, they were still selling cattle at 8PM and they are normally through by 5PM. It looks as if there is going to be a glut on the cattle market, which will cause prices to drop lower. With the shortage of hay, hay prices will increase. I think it is called supply and demand. It is just bad luck all around. Sort of a no-win situation… or so it seems. A no-win situation can always be turned around and always has been by the American farmer.

Some of the farmers have already moved their cattle to what was planned to be their hayfields because the cattle have already grazed the grass that was supposed to be summer grazing. Yes, sir, it is a dilemma for sure. The American farmer always survives… they have a special instinct and stick-to-itiveness that very few people of the general population are blessed with. The American farmer will find a way… always has, always will. I tip my hat to the American farmer.

I am sitting here in Bob and Gaye's Pickin' and Grillin' Parlor and thinking of my many blessings. As I look at the old farmhouse, it is hard to believe that it has provided shelter to someone for over 100 years. It has provided many memories, and a peaceful place to live my life for 45 years. I can't think of a place I would rather live. I look at the drought-stricken hayfield and I know that they will soon be nourished and everything will be fine in the end. Yes, sir, life is good. It is worth it to just live my life the way that I do.

The Lord is my Shepherd, I shall not want, He maketh me to lie down in green pastures, He leadeth me beside the still waters, He restoreth my soul. Yes sir, all will be fine. I'm covered. Bob

SPRING CLEANING

When I looked at the exterior of my workshop yesterday, it was as if I was seeing it for the first time. It looked totally different from what I remember building. It is a vinyl siding building that I built about 25 or 30 years ago. I use it just about every day. In the old days, there was a lot of work done in that building… these days, not so much, mainly piddling around with something.

I try to keep the inside fairly neat and orderly, but the outside was filthy. You see, it just slipped up on me. It had mildew, tree drippings and sap, and about any other kind of dirt you can think of. If you are around something every day, the changes come on gradually, and you simply do not notice it. After a while, it gets so bad that you cannot help but notice… and you ask yourself, "How did this happen?"

I got out the pressure washer and began work. It beat all I had ever seen as that building began to change its appearance. All of the years of built-up dirt and grime began to come off that building. The waste water was black. Now the building is back to its regular beige color. Looks as good a new.

That got me to thinking. Sometimes we do something… something that we know we shouldn't, but we do it anyway. You get by with it, and the next thing you know you are doing it over and over again. We get so accustomed to doing it, that we no longer realize that we are doing wrong. Just like that dirty building, it just slips up on us.

This is Spring… time for spring cleaning. I expect I need to take a close look at myself and wash off a few smudges. I ain't saying that you have any smudges, but you would be wise to do the same. No offense. You will look as good as new…. just like that building. bob

TACKINESS

When I was in high school, I worked at the Winn-Dixie as a stocker, bag boy, carry-out boy, cashier, janitor, and whatever else that needed doing.

I always enjoyed working on Saturday afternoon. You see, in those days the store was closed on Sunday so I was going to get a day off.

One of my favorite things was watching all the women shoppers with curlers in their hair on Saturday afternoon. Yes, sir, they sure did that… and by the dozens. I guess they were getting ready for Saturday night events or Sunday church services and wanted to look their best. The curlers needed to be in their hair for X number of hours… at least, that is my best guess as to why they did it.

The women who wore curlers were always in a hurry and only bought one or two things. They were probably picking up last minute items for their "big event" that night.

The curlers were mainly blue, pink, and white. The ladies that used curlers usually had a little cloth of some kind covering their heads. Some of the ladies used "bobby pins." Those women would usually have a hair net on their heads instead of one of those cloth coverings.

Women and girls from all walks of life did that every Saturday afternoon. Yes sir, there were rich, poor, blue collar, white collar, smart, dumb. Ford owners, and Cadillac owners......Tackiness had no boundaries.

It has worsened over the years. Nowadays, they wear pajamas with uncombed hair to the grocery store. Oh, well. bob

ENJOY THE RIDE

This morning was really good for me. Justin and I went to the morning Crawdad's game. That was our first father/son outing in a long time. For you out-of-towners, the Crawdads are a Class A ball team of the Texas Rangers. The game started at 10:30AM. That was an unusual starting time, but it gave people who normally work a second shift job the opportunity to see a game.

We had front row box seats right beside the Crawdad's dugout. They were great seats and we were up close and personal with all the action. The players on both teams were really good players who are intent on working their way to the majors. Most of them were from 19 to 21 years of age, with big dreams and visions of a major league career.

They think they are men, and they are, but to me they looked like children. That has something to do with me being a seasoned citizen, I guess. I remember when I was that age, I was serving one of two tours in Vietnam. I had big dreams and visions... some I realized, and some I didn't. We thought we were men, but now looking back, we were just boys doing a man's job.

I hope that all of the ball players I saw today make it to the majors, but most of them won't. I hope that every soldier works their way up to be a General or an Admiral, but most of them won't. I hope that the small business that you operate becomes a giant conglomerate, but most likely it won't. I hope that your job, whatever it may be, leads you to the top, but that is not likely to happen either. Only a few make it to the top.

It doesn't matter if you make it to the top rung of the ladder. Just keep climbing, and every time you fall, get back on that ladder. When you make it to the top, there is no way to go but down. Enjoy the climb, friends... that is where you will find your happiness and joy. bob

ONION SANDWICHES

Everyone around here is already talking about how they can't wait for their first home-grown tomato sandwich of the year... me being one of them.

This might seem strange to some of you (well probably not, coming from me), but I love plain old onion sandwiches, almost as well. Nothing like a sweet onion, fresh from the garden with mayo, salt, white bread, and pepper.

We usually peel a few fresh onions and put them in the fridge in a quart jar with a vinegar and water mixture. Two days ago, I got the onions and mayo out of the refrigerator and made myself a sandwich, and, my oh my, that thing was good.

Yesterday, Gaye was making herself a pimento cheese sandwich, and asked me, "What is an onion doing in the mayonnaise jar?" Thinking quickly, I said, "I think it has marinated long enough...I'll come and eat it now." No way would I admit that I put the unused part of the onion in the wrong jar. She, and many others worry enough about my mind going away, I do not need to give them any more food for thought. bob

GROWING UP

Sometimes on mornings like this, I like to think back to a kinder and gentler time. To me that was during the 50's when I was just a youngster attending elementary school.

My little town of Newton, NC was just a typical southern town. We had a town square with the court house being the center piece. That courthouse was surrounded by any type of store you can think of. We sure did not have any malls, shopping centers, or fast food places. We were kinda like Mayberry.

We did have department stores for all of our clothing needs. We could even put our foot into an X-ray machine at one of the department stores and look at our feet when we were buying a new pair of shoes. We had dime stores, grocery stores, hardware stores, novelty stores, movie theaters, pool rooms, drug stores and plenty of cafes. I loved my little town.

I particularly enjoyed attending elementary school and being with my friends all day. My friends at elementary school were sure a diverse bunch. Some were from the rich side of town and some lived on "the other side of the tracks". We didn't care... and probably did not know the difference. All I know is that we would play until dark when we got out of school.

Summer vacation was always a lot of fun. We kids would run all over town and would play until dark. The only thing we disagreed on was what was better... a Chevy or a Ford. Our parents usually knew where we were and did not worry about us. They knew we would be home at "suppertime." It was a time of innocence and naivety... a lot of both.

Our parents were the same way. They were all close friends. They were just trying to establish their place in the world and to carve out their little spot. My dad was a Southern Democrat who was happy when Eisenhower, a republican, became president in 1952. He knew that Eisenhower would do a good job for America.

When you become an adult, life becomes a lot more complicated. Everyone has their agenda... Christian, non-Christian, atheist, liberal, conservative, gay, straight, rich, poor, and well, you know all the things that separate us. It seems that "my" agenda is more important than "your" agenda... and I will not budge an inch. That is the reason that America is suffering such division these days.

I have no idea what we can do to become united once again... I just don't know. I try to be optimistic, but truthfully, I wonder if it is even possible. We have become accustomed to getting our way on every little thing and have become spoiled. Greed, stubbornness, and personal ego are at the top of the list of our problems.

We are better than this, or at least we once were. bob

COUNT YOUR BLESSINGS

Many of us are complaining about the hot weather as we sit in our homes in air-conditioned comfort. It is not like that for everyone.

Two days ago, Gaye asked me to stop by Walmart and pick up a few things on my way home from the Y. I got out of my truck and a noticed a truck with the hood up. Sitting beside the truck were two sweat-soaked men, surrounded by all kinds of tools. I asked them if they needed anything. They said, "No, we are just taking a break from putting this water hose on." Usually you just need a screwdriver to replace a water hose, but in this case, they had to remove all kinds of things to get to it. I could not help but think how hot it must be to them working on a hot engine on an asphalt parking lot. Someone later told me that asphalt temperature was 150 degrees and I do not doubt it. In addition to the things Gaye wanted, I got them two bottles of water. They were appreciative and said they had never been so hot in their lives. I can imagine.

On the way home, I encountered a work crew of inmates weed eating along the side of the road. I have always said that inmates need to work, but this could almost be considered cruel and inhumane punishment.

Things are not working out too well for me today. I have a flat tire on a tractor, a flat tire on a lawnmower, and a dead battery in the ATV. I was sweating through my clothes by the time I got the battery out… and that is an easy job and I was in the shade. I do not plan to fix the tires until later tonight when the sun goes down.

Before you complain about this heat, be sure to count your blessings. You could be employed as a roofer putting on an asphalt roof or maybe on a road crew. Be careful, everyone, and drink lots of water. I heard a warning that seniors need to stay in because of the air quality.

Count your many blessings, count them one by one. bob

TOMATOES

Tomatoes, tomatoes, and more tomatoes. We have been eating tomatoes non-stop for about six weeks and I am starting to get tired of them.

Do you remember last Spring when we were all anxiously awaiting our first tomato sandwich made with a homegrown tomato? Since that time, I have eaten approximately 643 tomato sandwiches and I do not desire another one for a while. We have canned tomatoes, pasta sauce, salsa, etc. We have given away bushels of tomatoes and only the Lord knows how many we have sliced and eaten with our meals. Enough is enough. It would not surprise me if some of you feel the same way.

For supper last night, Gaye made a TOMATO PIE. That was my first ever tomato pie and what a treat it was. You can find the recipe online, but here is Gaye's version:

Make a pie crust out of those crescent roll triangles that come in a can in the dairy case. Fill the pie crust with a mixture of tomatoes, onions, and basil. (We were out of basil and used oregano) Salt and pepper to taste. Top the mixture with a mixture of mayonnaise and shredded cheddar cheese. Bake at 350 for 30 minutes. Eat it while it is hot.

This pie is so good that it will make the show dog leave home. Try it. It is quick and easy to do. I wouldn't mind having another one for supper tonight. bob

MR. SCHUSSLER'S VW

This is a legendary story that goes back fifty-five years. People are still talking about it. About a month ago I was having a chicken salad sandwich at the H & W Drug Store, and a young man in his 20's or 30's asked me if I knew anything about this. Yeah, I did. I was one of the principals. Here goes…

When I was in the 9th grade, I had an English teacher named Ralph. Ralph was a pleasant and very nice man. In addition to teaching English, he taught Latin. He was also the Pastor of a Lutheran Church, Missouri Synod congregation in the area.

Ralph's car was a 1948 Plymouth. It was his prized possession, but the time had come to trade cars. He decided to trade for a 1961 Volkswagen Beetle. He ordered his new VW and that was all he ever talked about. It finally arrived and he was telling us all about it one day during class.

Steve Hollar and I asked him if we could go and look at it. He said, "Surely, my boys, it is parked on 6th Street." He said that he usually parked on Ashe Avenue in front of the school, but I decided to start parking on 6th Street because there was less traffic and it was unlikely that anyone would crash into it.

Steve and I took off running to see that fine car. Before we got out of the building, we encountered David Sims who was skipping class and was hiding on the stairs. David decided to go with us.

It was a nice car parked parallel to the curb. We looked it over carefully for about five minutes, and then decided to see if we could pick the car up and set it in the front yard of the house that was there... Well, we could and we did.

As we were walking back to the school, Ralph and the principal met us. It seems that the lady who lived in the house called the school and told on us. We went back to the car and put it back in its parking place.

When we got the car back in place, Ralph said, "I think it is shitty, S-H-I-T-T-Y (spelled out) of you boys to do this to my new car." Well, yes it was. We were wrong. We were just boys being boys. It was considered mischief.

The moral of the story is that Steve and I were not punished in any way, but they did something to David for skipping class. In this day and age, that would have probably been enough to get us suspended from school, or maybe charged with a felony. It was a kinder and gentler time.

For you, local people, that is exactly what happened. The story has been told and retold so many times that there are different versions, but this is the true version. I was there. bob

DRUGS... IT CAN HAPPEN TO ANYONE

About forty years ago I was going to tear down an old barn that was in ruins and beyond renovation. It was probably the first barn ever built on this property, over a century ago.

As I was looking around, the barn gave evidence of occupancy... cigarette butts, beer cans, an old blanket, etc. I asked my neighbor, "L", if he knew anything about it. He told me who was living there. The occupant was the son of a very prominent family in this area. His family had asked him to leave their home because he was stealing things from the home and selling them to get drug money. We knew the family well.

I waited until late that night to see if I could catch him at "home." Sure enough, he was there and began to truthfully tell me his story of drug use and addiction. It was a horrible story to hear. I thought about inviting him to stay with us, but I decided to leave him in the barn because of his thievery. It would have also been a bad example for our young son.

Gaye, in her motherly fashion, would take bread, peanut butter, beanie weenies, potted meat, crackers, etc. and leave in a stall for him. This went on until Fall faded into Winter and he just disappeared when the cold weather came.

A few weeks later he showed up at the house and said that he and some of his friends had a place to live and needed some fuel oil for the oil stove. Since diesel fuel and #2 heating oil are the same thing, I gave him 4 or 5 five-gallon cans of diesel fuel from my 250-gallon diesel fuel tank. He was very thankful, and that was the last time we saw him.

I remember attending his funeral a few years later and there was a Lynyrd Skynyrd record (I believe) in his casket with him. The record is unimportant, I just thought it was interesting.

Drug addiction can happen to anyone. Rich, poor, educated or uneducated. It is the worst cancer that our nation is facing. It has become so common that Americans have become complacent to it. Illegal drugs kill more people than ISIS.

If you are addicted to drugs, stand tall, hold your shoulders back, and be a man or woman, and SEEK HELP. Get out of denial. You will not only ruin your life, but also the lives of those around you. I have seen it happen too many times. Let's put those drug dealers (murderers) out of business. bob

GRAND LARCENY... GUILTY

This little story will give you a slice of life about living in the small southern town of Newton, NC in the 50's. This story involved Joe Cline, the grandfather of <u>Cindy Drum Gabriel</u>, so I will dedicate it to you, Cindy.

During those days, all of my friends (ages 12 and under) would run around the neighborhood all day long during the summer months and terrorize all the citizens... One of our favorite things to do was fish in a pond located near the old hospital in South Newton. The pond was also located adjacent to Cline's Floats. Cline's was the premier float builder in America, and they would haul floats all over the country to various parades.

Cline's had a lot of old cars, Jeeps, and trucks parked in a field near their facility. I do not remember if they left the keys in the vehicles or if they would start without a key... all I know is that when we got tired of fishing, we would go to that field and drive a certain World War ll era Jeep around and around in that field. We never asked permission to drive. Mr. Cline knew we were doing it and did not care.

One day David Sims and I were fishing and decided to drive the Jeep to town. I had a nickel and David had a dime. I was going to drive that Jeep to Smith's Drug Store and get two cokes and a candy bar. I drove that thing to town and parked in front of the drug store, and we got our soda pops and Reese Cup.

When we finished our treats, we got back into the Jeep, circled the square and were on the way to return that Jeep. The first thing I knew, the red, flashing light of a police car was behind me. I thought that Mr. Cline had called the police and they had an All-Points Bulletin out for me.

I pulled over and the policeman, Ivy Hass, exclaimed, "I might have known it was you." We explained to him what we had done. He told us to drive that Jeep back to Cline's, and he would follow us and then take me home to tell my Dad. BTW, the reason he stopped me was because the Jeep did not have a license plate.

When we got to Cline's, Mr. Cline came out to talk to the policeman AND us. He told us to stay in the field when driving that Jeep, and not to get on the highway. We then got into the police car for our ride home. I remember feeling sick to my stomach. I knew Dad would "wear me out like a new ground," then I would get booked and taken to jail.

When the policeman got me home, Dad was waiting for us on the front porch. Mr. Cline had called Dad and told him what to expect. Nothing happened. In fact, Dad and the policeman were laughing about it.

I was expecting to be charged with grand theft auto, driving without a license (I was 12), and driving without registration. There were no charges whatsoever. It was a different time and a different place. I still miss those days. We were just boys being boys. bob

HEROES

What is a hero? I don't know for sure. Webster could tell me if I wanted to look it up, but I have my own old-fashioned belief. I guess it is a matter of personal interpretation anyway.

I was listening to a sports talk radio program one-night last week. They were discussing the Olympic athlete who claimed that he was robbed while on the town in Rio. The truth came out that he was not robbed, but instead he had trashed a service station in Rio. I have yet to figure out what that was all about.

Anyway, one of the radio callers said a few detrimental things about that athlete. The host of the show said, "You can't talk like that about an Olympic hero." The next morning, I heard that athlete say that he was "intoxicated and over- exaggerated what had happened." Well, I guess that explains it all to some people... but not me. It seems to me that he is a drunk and a liar. Not exactly what I consider an Olympic Hero.

I know an Olympic Hero who never got credit for it. In fact, his life was ruined because of it. Do you remember Richard Jewel? Richard Jewel was the security guard who discovered a bomb during the 1996 Olympics in Atlanta. He evacuated many people from the area, saving many lives and injuries. He did not get credit for it.

Instead, the media crucified him. They said that he planted the bomb, was seeking recognition, and was trying to be important. They were relentless in their pursuit of him. They camped out in his front yard, making him a prisoner in his own home. What a shame. They had no proof.

It turned out that Richard was not involved, but his life was never the same. It was just another example of our so-called media ruining someone's life. He died a few years ago without ever receiving recognition. He deserved a Presidential Award of some kind.

I know that I am old and out of touch, but Richard Jewel is what I consider to be an American Olympic Hero. bob

THE GAS SHORTAGE

I remember the gasoline shortage in the 70's. Most stations didn't have any gas, and those that did would only sell you four or five gallons.

One day at work I was concerned that I might not have enough fuel to get home, let alone get back to work tomorrow. I was talking to a fellow employee, and he told me that he was driving his Honda 250cc motorcycle because it got almost 100 miles to the gallon. I told him that, "I would love to have one of those things." He told me that he had two of them, and he would sell me either one for $750 dollars.

We went to lunch together that day and decided that we would ride double on his motorcycle with me being the driver. We were driving through Newton, and the stoplight in front of Citizens Savings and Loan was red so I had to stop. After the light changed, I drove two blocks and had to stop at the stoplight in front of the EXXON station. I turned to say something to him and he was gone. The way I was jerking that motorcycle around, I felt like I had thrown him off and he was somewhere dead on the pavement.... or at least bleeding profusely.

As I went back to see if I could find him, he was standing in front of Citizens Savings and Loan. It seems that when I was stopped there earlier, he, being a tall, lanky fellow, stood up to stretch his legs and I drove right out from under him and left him standing in the street. Neither he nor I ever lived that down.

I decided right then that I didn't need a motorcycle. The Lord provided then and He will now. bob

PATRIOTISM

I, Bobby Earl Marlowe, do solemnly swear that I will support and defend the Constitution of the United States against all enemies, foreign and domestic, that I will bear true faith and allegiance to the same.

The above is part of the oath that I took when I joined the US Navy on August 6, 1965. That oath was not just for the four years that I served on active duty, but for life.

Here are some mottos that I still adhere to:

Not for Self but Country. (That is the unified motto of the Armed Forces.)

Honor, Courage, Commitment. (US Navy Core Values)

I have not yet begun to fight. (John Paul Jones)

Damn the torpedoes, full speed ahead. (Admiral David Farragut)

Some people think heroes are fearless. No, heroes are afraid, but they do it anyway. bob

MY MISTAKE

This morning, for some reason, I got up at 4AM. Don't ask me to explain it, I just did. I had a nice breakfast of bacon, eggs, grits, toast, and coffee and went back to bed.

When I got back up, I went to the Y and had a nice workout. When I left the Y, I was really hungry. It occurred to me that it had been 6 hours since I had eaten.

I stopped at Bojangles and got a Cajun filet biscuit and a tea for $4.15. When I got to the window, I paid with a 10-dollar bill.

The lady gave me my change of $5.85 and then went to get my tea. I squirmed around and got the $.85 in my pocket. She then came back with my tea. I reached for it with the five-dollar bill still between my fingers. She broke out into a big smile and said, "thank you very much," as she took my five-dollar bill and handed me my tea. There was no way that I could disappoint her and tell her that I did not mean to give her the five-dollar bill. Lesson learned, but I left with both of us feeling good about it. bob

MY HALLOWEEN COSTUME

Well, my tender feelings are damaged beyond repair and my self-esteem is gone. I think I am going to lock the main gate to the house and stay at home for the rest of my life… I will never get over this. Gloom, despair, agony, deep dark depression, and excessive misery have set in.

I am not much of a fan of Halloween. My lovely friend, Sudie Hamilton Brown, suggested that I would like Halloween better if I would put on a costume. Then another dearly beloved, sweet and charming friend, Sharon Freeman Fowler, told me to just put on a pair of overalls for Trunk or Treat at my church. Well, that is what I did.

My fellow church members did not say anything to me about my overalls. They were accustomed to seeing me dressed like that. But here is where the trouble came in:

A 20ish Mexican woman with a husband and 2 children pointed at me and their faces lit up. I smiled at them and spoke kindly to them as I welcomed them to our church. She said, "I would like to find some clothes like you are wearing for my husband to wear next Halloween."

Everything seemed fine and then it occurred to me that I dress like a Halloween character all the time. No, sir. I will not leave the farm again, and will keep the gate locked so no one can get in. I will need a lot of professional help to get over this. bob

VETERANS DAY

I did not celebrate Veterans Day as I usually do. Most of the time, I put my picture on Facebook from way back then and tell the dates of my service, etc. Instead, I stayed off the internet all day and watched a 3 or 4-hour documentary on TV entitled, "Vietnam" in HD. It brought back many memories from the years I was there ('67 to '69).

It was mentioned on that show that the Vietnam veterans were not met with ticker-tape parades, etc. when they came home… but with scorn. That is true, but most of us didn't expect a great celebration. We thought that going to war was simply our duty and a part of life. All we wanted was to come home and get on with our lives.

Many veterans spoke of getting spit on and abused verbally upon arrival in the States, but none of that happened to me. I did have an experience in the San Francisco Airport as I awaited a flight to bring me home… A door slammed, or there was a loud noise of some kind, and I "hit the deck." People sitting near me laughed, and I took it in stride and laughed as well. There were certain times in Vietnam that I felt scared, but apparently, I was wound up like a clock the whole time and did not know it at the time… Many of my friends said they were the same way when they returned stateside… Evidently, we became so accustomed to feeling like that… maybe we considered it as a normal feeling. I do not know. It is hard for me to explain.

As I watched the TV show that I mentioned earlier, I was reminded of my friends. I remember faces, but not many names anymore. God Bless them all, wherever they are… and God Bless You. Yes, sir, I am a proud Veteran. Duty, Honor, Courage. bob

HARTSOE'S BODY SHOP·

I got a message from <u>Sarah Hartsoe McLeod</u> wanting me to write a story about Hartsoe's Body Shop in Newton, NC. Sarah has lived in the Philippines for years helping those folks. Her brothers Harrill, Bobby, and Eddie worked at the shop. Bobby and Eddie were twins and three years older than me. Harrill was older than the twins but I do not know how much older.

Back in 1964, Hartsoe's was THE body shop in Newton, NC. They had a reputation for doing quality work at discount prices. That is exactly the kind of business that I liked.

I was in high school at the time and my car was a 1961 Volkswagen Beetle. It had a few minor body issues that I wanted to have repaired. I took it by Hartsoe's to get a quote. I will never forget that the price was $100. I knew that was a good deal, but if you do not have the money… what are you going to do? I told them that I could not afford it… but would try to save the money.

They told me that I could work on it myself and that they would guide me and that I could use their tools. You could not beat that. I would work on the car for an hour or two after school on the days that I did not have to work at the Winn-Dixie and soon had the car repaired. They did not charge me a penny.

Now let's fast forward to about 2008. I bought an antique Allis Chalmers tractor that I wanted to rebuild as a hobby. There was a great big dent in the gas tank. I could not locate a replacement gas tank and I could not figure out how to repair it without breaking a seal.

I remembered from almost 50 years earlier that Harrill invented a tool that would work....so I took the tank off and rode to North Newton to see if he still had that tool. He said that he did have the original tool, but it was now being reproduced, and body shops all over the country were using it.

I told him who I was, and he remembered me by asking, "Are you the one who had the blue Volkswagen?" I told him that I was. We got the tool out and in a matter of minutes had the dent out of that gas tank. I applied a little Bondo to make it perfectly smooth, and sanded and primed it.

When I got through, I asked Harrill, "How much do I owe you?" He replied, "Not a thing, you never have paid me a cent and there is no use to start now."

Harrill closed the shop a year or two ago, he just aged out. One of the twins died in a truck accident in the 70's, and the other is in poor health.

Of course, they ran that shop as a for-profit business, and I am sure they made a lot of money... but they sure were good, kind, and fair to everyone. Business owners of today could take a lesson from the Hartsoes. This high school boy will never forget them. Thanks, guys. bob

A NICE LADY

Sometimes we are lucky to be in the right place at the right time. Yesterday, Gaye and I dined at Wendy's for lunch and met a wonderful little woman eating at the table beside of us.

She was sitting in the back corner of the restaurant and there was no one sitting near her. I could just tell by looking at her that she was someone that I would like to know. We sat down beside her and struck up a conversation.

She was 88 years old and had been a widow for 7 years. Her husband died on December 26th from a fall at home. She told us all about that episode and then started showing us pictures of her family and told us how proud she was of them. She was excited about Christmas and looking forward to being with her family. She told us that she now lives alone, can still drive, and gets along just fine. She also testified about her faith in God.

She said she was on her way to Walmart to buy groceries. We told her that we were also going there to buy a few things. When she got up from her seat, we noticed that she was walking with a cane and was having trouble carrying her tray to the disposal place. We were getting ready to go, and Gaye took her tray, and I got to walk her to her car.

We saw her at Walmart, and every time we crossed paths we would speak and smile. She was the sweetest and kindest little thing that I have seen in a long time. She just had a sweet smile that made you feel warm and cuddly, and that all is right in the world.

We intentionally checked out right behind her. We just wanted to be with her. Among the things that she bought was a large can of chicken and dumplings that she was going to donate to a "can ministry" that collects canned food for those not so fortunate. The last time we saw her she was on the way to the pharmacy with her $20.91 worth of groceries to get her medicine.

That lady was probably the most inspiring and uplifting person I have met this year. We were truly blessed to get to meet her. I do not think it was an accident. bob

GOOD FRIENDS

Josh, TJ, Randy, and I had plans to move some bulls around today. Josh's bull was at Randy's house and we were going to take it back to Josh's. My bull was at the other farm, and we were going to bring it to the home farm.

When I woke up this morning, I felt as if I was catching the crud that Gaye had. I sent them a text and told them that they were more than welcome to use my truck and trailer to move Josh's bull, and I would move mine after church tomorrow. The wind was blowing and I did not want to be in it.

Josh and TJ came by to get the truck and trailer and came in the house to visit for a while. They hooked up the trailer and left.

I was looking out the window a few hours later, and I saw Josh at the corral unhooking the trailer. I called him and told him to leave it hooked up because I would be using it in the morning. He said, "I forgot about that." Josh got back to the house and said, "I don't follow directions very well." I noticed that he had unhooked the trailer anyway. He said, "Your bull has been back at the house for a couple hours." I had no idea that they had gone over to our other farm and brought the bull home.

Good friends are hard to beat. I sure do appreciate things like that. bob

ANOTHER GOOD FRIEND

As you age, you experience many changes… some good, some not so good…

On Tuesday, Gaye and I were out and about running a few errands. I asked Gaye where she would like to have lunch. She said that she would like to have a good old-fashioned hot dog or hamburger from a home-owned restaurant, not some fast food or franchise place...

I remembered a place called Sonny's in the Highland area of Hickory from about 20 years ago. I didn't even know if it was still in operation.

We got to the non-descript building that is old and looks like it has seen its better days. We entered and it had the same old lunch counter with the same cracked Formica, the same old bar stools with the same torn upholstery. We sat at a worn-out, wobbly table, also with cracked Formica and the same old wobbly chairs. The floor was concrete with loose tiles....and of course, the aroma of burned grease still wafted through the air.

Nothing had changed in those 20 years. I was never a regular there, but always enjoyed it when I did go. My favorite was the country style steak.

As we entered the back door, the first thing I saw was the owner sitting at a table, taking the many "call in" orders and also serving as cashier. I guess she aged out from standing behind that hot grill.

When she saw me, both of our eyes lit up, and she said, "I was just thinking about you last week." That surprised me because I really never "knew" her. She was just the lady who fixed that good country style steak.

We talked for a few minutes and it was as if we were continuing an old conversation from yesterday, but it had been 20 years.

The building had not changed, but the menu was just a little bit different. She no longer has the country style steak. She said that it now cost $7 a pound and she would have to pay her customers to eat it.

Yes, things change as you age but old friends and acquaintances stay the same. I enjoyed my cheeseburger and Gaye enjoyed her dollar hot dog, but most of all I enjoyed my old friend. Lord, when my work on earth is done, just grant me one old friend. bob

ATTITUDE

It amazes me how people react to things. Some take it in stride while others act so negatively and act as if they are the only one in the world with a problem.

Gaye and I have two friends suffering from cancer. Let me tell you about them.

One needs surgery, but it is going to be a while before he can get it. He first has to go through Radiation Therapy five days a week for six weeks, and Chemo Therapy one day each week for six weeks. Then he must wait four weeks until they can do a Pet Scan to see if he has reached the point that they can do surgery. In the mean-time, he has a feeding tube and his food is delivered 15 hours a day, directly into his intestines. We visited with him and his wife for a little while after church on Sunday.

Our other friend has had recurring cancer for several years. She will be undergoing a lot of testing in the next two weeks to try to find out everything that is going on with her. Lots of doctors and about every X-ray that you can think of is on the agenda. They think that the cancer might be in her brain now because she is losing her eyesight and cannot even read. We visited with her and her husband for an hour or so today.

If anyone has a reason to whine, be bitter, or complain, I guess these two do. However, they are both positive, up-beat, and friendly. When I go to visit them, I go to try to encourage them. Instead, I end up being encouraged.

I think attitude is everything and these two are going to end up beating that thing. bob

LIVE TRIUMPHANTLY

I see the world changing every day... I do not know what to think about it. This is just not how I was reared.

There are mobs running wild all over the world....and they call it a protest. Other people are hiding within themselves. Other folks are going to their "safe place" to be with like-minded people. Other people say they are afraid. Other folks have just given up and say they cannot function because of stress. I just do not understand all of this.

I read on the internet today that the use of anti-anxiety drugs has exploded. Of course, everything you read on the internet is not true, but I believe that to be true.

I realize, and those of you who know me, know that I live in the 1800's. There are good and bad aspects of living like I do. I realize that, but I ain't changing. The rest of you can do whatever you want to do, but I am not going to let anyone upset my joy.

All I can say is that God did not give me, or any of you a spirit of fear. Live boldly and triumphantly. bob

A NEW FRIEND

I don't know if it is like this all over America, but here in North Carolina you can end up having a conversation in the grocery store aisle with someone you have never met… and end up learning all kinds of things.

This morning Gaye and I were smelling tomatoes at the grocery store trying to find some that had an aroma. A man of about my age, or a little older, walked up and started a conversation.

Him: You must be richer than you look if you can afford those tomatoes.

Me: Well, yes sir, I am. Everyone says I look homeless. If you look homeless, but actually have a home, I guess you are richer than you look.

He then proceeded to tell me about himself. He was a truck driver in Vietnam, but never saw any action. His wife died last year, and he already has a girlfriend who has a cattle farm. He helped her take a load to the sale this past week and the price is still down. He bought some grapes last week at Food Lion for $3 a pound and the ones on the bottom of the bag were not "fit to eat." It made him mad, but he didn't take them back to the store because he was afraid, he would "act up" and lose his Christian witness.

He left me with this: Slapping his pants pocket, he said, "I have Jesus in my heart and a gun in my pocket." (My new favorite saying). I liked him and believe we could be friends. bob

THE KEEPER OF THE GATE

I call her the "Keeper of the Gate." She just does it without being asked….and it makes things better and easier for me. Let me explain.

The hardest thing about feeding cattle is climbing down and then back up on the tractor to open and close the gates. Here is the basic procedure for giving hay to cattle: You go to where the hay is stored, get on the tractor, and run the hay spear that is on the front-end loader into a round bale of hay. Then you start driving to the feedlot. You get to the gate, climb down from the tractor, open the gate, climb back onto the tractor, drive the tractor through the gate, climb back down off the tractor, close the gate behind you, climb back onto the tractor, drive to the feedlot, and drop the bale of hay. You then repeat the whole process as you return with the tractor. You spend most of your time climbing onto and off the tractor to open the gates.

Without asking her, Gaye goes to the gate and opens it for me. She then stands there until I return and opens it again for me to pass back through. She started doing that for me several years ago. She is never deterred....no matter what the weather. Snow, rain, freezing temperatures or whatever.... she automatically shows up. It makes it easy for me. I never leave the tractor.

We are all going to approach another gate one of these days. That gate is called the Pearly Gates. St. Peter will be the "Keeper of that Gate." He will not be quite as lenient as Gaye. Some will be allowed to enter.... others will not. I have made arrangements to gain entrance at that gate... hopefully, you have too.

By the way, I am spoiled rotten. bob

DON'T LET IT SLIP UP ON YOU

Sometimes when things go wrong, we often feel that it is not all that important and let it go. Sometimes that works out and sometimes it doesn't.

I have a tractor that has been leaking power steering fluid for a couple of years. It started out being a "slow leak." It would be a lot easier to add more power steering fluid than to properly fix it. That is what I did. After all, it only uses a $4 bottle of power steering fluid a year. To repair the power steering would probably cost $300, and it is a difficult repair. This year it used about 3 bottles of power steering fluid. Things are getting worse to say the least. Pretty soon it will probably be leaking a bottle per week. When you let things go, they usually get worse.

I will soon be moving my cows across the road to a new pasture. Before I move them, there is work to do. I must ride the fence lines and look for loose and broken barbed wire and broken or rotten posts. They must be repaired or cows will be running all over the community. In this case, things can go wrong quickly.

While riding the fence, I look for cedar trees coming up under the fence. You have all seen large cedar trees around a pasture fence. That is not a good thing. As I am riding the fence line, I carry a pair of loppers with me and cut them off while they are still small. You see, as the cedar tree grows it will do damage to the fence. It can pull the staples and fasteners off the fence post. I have even seen them pull posts out of the ground. If you do not pay attention, it can sneak up on you and the first thing you know, you have major damage.

Sometimes we decide not to go to church. After all, it is such a pretty morning and the golf course or the lake are calling. Pretty soon you are playing golf or fishing every Sunday morning and forget that you should be in church. It just sneaks up on you.

Sin works the same way. Sometimes we all do some little thing that we shouldn't and we get by with it. The first thing you know, you are doing that thing more often, and in a more, risky manner. That is a dangerous thing and soon you do it without realizing you are doing wrong. Yep, again, it just sneaks up on you.

Don't let these things sneak up on you. It is very dangerous. Be careful. bob

SLOW DOWN

Sometimes we get out of sorts and somehow, we forget what is important and valuable in life. At least I do, but I am trying to do better.

This morning I got to the Y at 9:15AM. Before I got to my first machine, a fellow stopped me and wanted to hear my opinion of Trump's speech last night. Since I do not watch the news or political events, I did not know anything about it, but took time to hear his opinion and thoughts on the matter. I then walked to the first machine and sat down and adjusted the weights.

As soon as I got the weights adjusted, a fellow of my age walked up to me and wanted to talk. It seems his son who lives out of state has been diagnosed with a rare kind of brain cancer. He explained how he had three sons and two have already died. He went on to explain how it looked as if he was going to lose another one. It just doesn't seem fair for a parent to outlive a child, but with tears in both of our eyes, I did everything I could to comfort him.

In the midst of that conversation, I girl came up behind me and wanted to talk about another unrelated topic. We talked for a few minutes and I resumed my conversation with the man who has the son with cancer.

As soon as we finished that conversation, here comes another fellow wanting to know my thoughts on the new NASCAR format.

I liked it and told him why. He said he was just not sure about it yet. We finished that conversation and he walked away.

As soon as he walked away, another fellow walked up to tell me something and to ask a question. As soon as finished, here comes another girl who wanted to check in.

I looked at the clock on the wall and it was 10:15AM. I had not lifted one weight or taken one step on the treadmill.... and I had been there an hour. Oh, well.

That was fine with me. In my earlier life, the old Alabama song, "I'm in a Hurry to Get Things Done" was my theme song.

I know that many young people and some of you seniors will not understand this, but as you get older you realize that time and your friends and family are your greatest assets on earth. We all need to love our friends and family, and to share our time. bob

FAMILY FUNDRAISER, DONATIONS ACCEPTED

Most of you are probably doing quite well. Of course, you have problems… but everyone does. But do you know what, it can turn around at the snap of a finger.

I was on the way to Rogers Mill in Taylorsville this morning to buy some cow feed and eggs. As I rode by the old hospital, there was a young lady standing there holding a sign that said, "Family Fundraiser, Donations Accepted." I did not stop but proceeded on to Rogers Mill, but I couldn't get them off my mind. Was this some kind of fraudulent thing or was the family really in need? I thought that it would be better to stop and give a donation on the way home. My simple way of thinking was, "It will be better to help them whether they need it or not." I will get a blessing either way.

When I stopped, I asked the young lady what kind of hardship she is enduring. I had my hand hanging out of the window of the truck and the little 2-year old girl came up and held my finger. Shoot, that made it worth stopping for.

The lady told me that she lost everything… EVERYTHING in a fire, this past Monday. I remembered reading about that. She told me that she is in need of everything… clothing, furniture, money… in other words, everything it takes to rebuild her household. It touched this old man's tender heart and made me count my many blessings. bob

HOME OWNED BUSINESSES

I like the simple life….and I like to be around like-minded people.

When I worked, the thing I dreaded most was being called into a meeting. When you put a bunch of people together in a room around a big long table, a simple problem becomes complicated. There was always some long-winded person sitting there who liked to hear himself/herself speak. That person would usually go on and on and on with a bunch of gibberish. That person would always use the PC words that were in vogue at the time. There was always a collective sigh of relief when that person finally shut up. No conclusion was ever reached in those meetings and, finally, after 4 or 5 meetings, someone would be empowered to take care of the situation. They should have empowered someone in the first place. ("Empowered" was one of the words that the long winded-person often used.) I guess that is the way it is in the corporate world so that the blame could be shared among many.

I do as much business as I can with small, home owned companies. Things are so simple when dealing with those people. They do not need a committee to solve a problem. This morning Gaye and I went to a home-owned store. I got some farm products and Gaye got some cabbage plants. I gave the cashier my debit card and it would not work. Someone standing there said that a car had torn down a telephone pole and that is why my card would not work. What to do? It was simple. The cashier told me to come back and pay later. She emphasized for me not to make a special trip. I didn't sign any papers or anything. I just left. Try that at Walmart. bob

FORGIVENESS

Yesterday morning Gaye and I were checking fences on the summer pasture. I haven't been to or even seen that pasture in 3 or 4 months. As we were riding the utility vehicle to that pasture, I noticed hoof prints all over the earthen dam around the pond. I could not quite figure it out. My cows are fenced out of that area.

When we got to the summer pasture, I saw the problem. There was a small group of unfamiliar cows on that pasture. My initial thought was, "I see a good profit in this." (Just kidding, I would never sell someone else's cows.) As soon as the cows saw us, they took off running and ran through a place in the fence that they had torn up. They knew they weren't supposed to be there. Well, I forgive them. We all fall short sometimes. I have had cows get out myself. It just happens. If they want out, they will get out.

I thought of Peter in the Bible. I got to portray Peter in a little skit with our Pastor. After the resurrection, Jesus and Peter were on the beach together and Jesus forgave Peter for denying Him three times. If Jesus can forgive Peter, I can sure forgive those cows.

I plan to fix that fence this morning when the rain stops. I might even go in the rain. After all, a little rain never hurt anyone. When you get a little rain in your life, dry off and keep on going.
bob

NEVER JUDGE A BOOK...

Yesterday an interesting thing happened while I was in Tractor Supply getting some fencing stuff.

A fellow walked up to me and said, "Bob, do birds change colors as they age?" I told him that I did not know… all the while wondering how he knew my name. I decided that in small southern towns like Mayberry and Taylorsville that it is not uncommon to know someone and them not know you.

He followed me as I was walking to the check out. He then asked, "How is Gaye getting along?" I told him that she was next door at Walmart getting some produce. He then asked me if I minded if he went to Walmart to talk to her. He said he would like to have a can of coffee and maybe Gaye would buy it for him. I replied, "Gaye doesn't like to be disturbed while buying groceries." By this time, I could tell that the lad had issues that needed treatment. I did buy him a candy bar at Tractor Supply. That was the biggest candy bar I had ever seen

He followed me to the truck and I asked him how he knew Gaye and me… He said that 2 years ago Gaye and I were in McDonald's with three children and that I bought him a coffee and a hamburger. He said "You remember me… Mark?" Yes, I did remember that incident.

I understand why he is unemployed. If I were a HR Manager, I doubt that I would even consider him for a job. But you know what, the old saying, "Never judge a book by the cover" comes to mind. He seemed physically fit, and with a memory like that… I am sure there is something he could do well if someone could see through his actions and appearance and give him an opportunity. bob

PRECONCEIVED NOTIONS

I was talking to a friend of mine this morning, and she told of an experiment that they did when she was a counselor at a high school. They made Jell-O out of unflavored gelatin and added unflavored cake coloring to it. Naturally, it had no taste. They would ask someone to taste the "red" and then ask them what flavor it was. They would always say cherry or strawberry. When they tasted the "green", they would always say "lime." It had no taste, but they were judging it by the color, not taste, as they were supposed to. Preconceived notions.

One time in the 80's I was having lunch with a friend at a cafeteria. When we got to the desserts, we both got a piece of the coconut cream pie. We sat down to eat and Bill scoffed his food down like it was his last meal. When I got to my coconut cream pie, it was not coconut cream pie. I did not know what it was. I asked Bill, who had already eaten his, "What kind of pie was that, Bill?" "Coconut cream," he replied. I said "It's NOT coconut cream pie, but I can't distinguish the flavor." When the waitress came around to fill our tea, she told me it was peanut butter. Preconceived notions.

I bought a new suit at a fine, high-dollar men's store when our son got married. I was wearing shorts, a stretched-out t-shirt, and tennis shoes. The clerk looked me up and down and asked, "And just what is your budget?" Most people would have gotten angry, but I felt sorry for her. Such a shallow person. Preconcei-ved notions.

It amazes me how so many people know so much about the book, and they haven't even read it yet. Preconceived notions. bob

STANDING OVATION

In the summer of 1958 when I was twelve, I enjoyed hanging around the local ball park where the American Legion and our Class D baseball team played in Newton, NC. To me, that sta-dium was a magnificent wooden structure, rivaling Yankee Sta-dium.

I became friends with the groundskeeper, a high school boy by the name of Turbyfill. He had what I thought was the perfect job. His duties were to mow the field twice a week with a large riding mower, and to "drag" the infield before each game. Both of those duties involved "driving." There was nothing a 12-year old boy likes better than driving. I could not think of a better job. Actually, it was THE perfect job.

At one point during the summer, the Turbyfill boy needed a week off, and luckily for me, the manager of the American Le-gion, Tubby Benfield, allowed me to fill-in for the week.

It was a win-win situation for me. My salary was $5 for the week... plus all the hot dogs and popcorn I could eat at the games... and I got to drive. Shoot, I would have done it for free.

My favorite part of the job was dragging the infield. Instead of using a four-wheeler with a leveling and smoothing device like they do now, my leveling device was a '49 Chevy, 6-cylinder, straight drive with an old mattress tied to the rear bumper.

On this particular night, the stands were full because of a doubleheader. Some of my friends wanted to ride with me as I "drug the field" between games. As we were approaching 2nd base, one of my friends said, "Stomp it, Bobby"...and I did.

I stomped it, quickly changed into second gear... and lost control. I spun out into left center field. Dust and sod were flying everywhere. The car clunked to a stop. Before I could get it restarted, Tubby ran onto the field, and at the top of his voice yelled, "You're fired!!!" Nothing worse than being fired in front of 1000 people.

Embarrassed, dejected, unemployed, and ashamed, I walked off the field to the standing ovation of the large crowd. I actually had to laugh at myself. I can still hear the roar of the crowd, and in my mind's eye I can see everyone waving at me. Needless to say, my working career did not get off to a good start.

I never did get my $5, but I did eat plenty of hotdogs and popcorn.

Just another memory of an old guy who still remembers the old days. I guess it is a matter of perspective, but I believe we had more fun than kids of today. bob

LIVE GENEROUSLY

Everywhere I go I seem to see more, unhappy, frowning faces than I do smiling faces. Some of those people seem dissatisfied with life when you talk to them. I can't quite figure it out. I think they are dissatisfied with themselves. You can see a hollow look in their eyes and on their faces.

The old Porter Wagoner song comes to mind. The first verse goes like this, "How many times have you heard someone say, if

I had his money, I could do things my way." Happiness, joy and satisfaction do not come from money or other things… but from within.

It seems that everyone wants a bigger house or car, more fame, more attention, better job, etc. They expect life to always be perfect and when that doesn't happen, they become dissatisfied and depressed… at least that is my observation. I feel sorry for those people. They can never get enough.

Life is what you make of it….it is up to you. Most of us do not have that many "big" days in our lives. You don't just get a new car or a new home every day, so try to find satisfaction with what you have. Enjoy the little everyday events… things like a mater' sammich, fresh from the garden, or a cold glass of water on these hot days. Cherish the little things and show love to everybody. Live generously. bob

CHANGES

It is amazing how things have changed in the last 20 or 25 years. It was hard for some of us seasoned citizens to adjust. Some of us grew up without lights or running water.

Do you remember when cell phones first became popular in the 90's? Many of you, including me said, "I will never have one of those things." Now I cannot ever remember all of the ones I have had.

Oh, and bottled water. I said, "I will never pay a dollar for a bottle of water because I can get it free at home." Well, I had to eat crow on that one too… we now buy it by the case.

And fax machines. I remember when I would fax a document to someone, I would always call them and ask if they got it. They would also call me when they sent me one. We just did not trust those new-fangled things.

Computers.... "Why in the world would I want one of those things in my home... what would I do with it?" Yep, eating crow again. I have probably had at least 10 and could not do without them. They have become an important part of most of our lives.

Can't forget cable TV. Why would I pay to watch TV when I can get 3 channels free with an antenna? Well, I have never had cable TV because it took them a long time to run lines in my part of the country... but I did buy one of those tacky, unsightly 6 or 8-foot dishes. Some of y'all probably remember them. Now I have a small dish and pay over $100 a month. I never would have believed that I would pay to listen to the radio either... but I do.

Oh, goodness, I would never shop online. That was out of the question. "After all, you cannot trust those online merchants." Online shopping and banking have become a part of my life. Very few days go by that I do not order online...usually from Amazon. I think it is interesting that my son ordered a few small items from Amazon earlier this week, and it was delivered in 8 hours. Amazing.

I can hardly wait to see what is next. bob

KILLING HORNETS

One Saturday morning, my cousin David Sims called asking for my help. He said that his in-laws with some young children from Michigan were coming to visit and stay a few days and were due to arrive that afternoon. He further explained that there was a hornets nest in a shrub in his front yard. He was afraid that some of the youngsters would be playing around the pool in their bathing suits and get stung by the hornets. He said that he had some hornet spray, but was terrified to spray them, and wanted to see if I would do it for him. Of course, I said I would.

I got to his house an hour or so later wearing shorts, t-shirt, and flip flops. He insisted that I wear some of his outerwear to help protect me. I agreed.

(You need to use your imagination and your visualization skills for the rest of this post.)

We went into the house on this hot August morning and we proceeded to dress me for this adventure. David was much larger than me, but we thought his clothes that he was going to provide for me to wear would be fine. David was about 6'4" and weighed probably 275 and I was 6' and weighed about 200.

First, he put a long sleeve wool sweat shirt on me. We then put on the matching wool pants. Next, I put on a pair of his boots.

We then went to the garage and found an old pair of gloves for me to wear. Our next step was to duct tape the shirt sleeves around the gloves and the pants around the boots to keep the hornets from getting inside my clothes. We also duct taped the shirt to the pants to keep the pants from falling down. I was a beautiful sight to behold.

Everything was covered except my head. He did not have a ski mask or anything, but we finally figured out what to do. (visualize) We would duct tape a swimming pool net around my head. Yeah, that should work....and yes, we did it.

He ran into the house as I began my task of spraying the hornets. I thought to myself, "I hope that no one comes by here who knows me and sees this." There I was...... standing in the front yard with a swimming pool net with a 6-foot handle duct taped around my neck.

As I stood there with my back to the road trying to figure out how to attack the hornets, someone said, "Bob, what are you doing with a swimming pool net on your head?" I turned to see who it was. It was his mail person, Catherine Huffman, a friend of mine. I walked to her truck and said, "Catherine, if you tell anyone about this, I will make up some stuff and tell on you." She was laughing hysterically as she drove away.

I did the job and all went well. The hornets were dead and I did not get stung.

When I got to church the next morning, people that I hardly knew were wanting to hear the story about me and the swimming pool net around my head. Catherine must have told everyone she saw and those people told others. The story spread throughout the area very quickly. This story brought a lot of laughter to people around here for a long time. Hope you enjoyed it. bob

WHAT HURTS WORSE?

There have always been questions going around to which we may never know the answer. Things like, what came first the chicken or the egg? Shoot, I don't know and really do not care. I am just glad that we have both.

The question that has been going around for years and seems to have reared its ugly self on us again is, "What hurts worse.......having a baby or getting kicked in the nuts?" That is an easy one. Carl Rector, my old cowboy friend, and I figured that one out many years ago. We often sat around in the heat of the day or the cool of the evening and pored over these things. Carl is gone now, and I have to figure them out by myself. I know you are all just dying to know the answer to the question. When you hear the simplicity of it, you will all snap your finger and say, "Dang, that was easy, why didn't I think of that?"

It hurts worse to get kicked in the nuts than to have a baby. Let me explain. Quite often, about a year after giving birth a lady will say, "I would like to have another baby." I have never been sitting around with a bunch of guys, even half-drunk guys, and out of the blue one of them says, "I would like for someone to kick me in the nuts today."

Now, let's put that question to rest. bob

WAITING FOR THE MAILMAN

At about 11AM, I would look up the road to see if he was coming. If he wasn't coming, I would sit on the porch and keep a sharp lookout for him. I was looking for, Mr. Dan, our mailman. The year was about 1953.

When he came into sight, I couldn't wait. I would take off running to meet him. "Mr. Dan, Mr. Dan, have you got anything for me?" No, Bobby, I don't have a thing today," he would often reply. That would be our routine just about every day until........

"Mr. Dan, Mr. Dan, do you have anything for me today?" "Let me see, Bobby, I think I have one in here for you from Battle Creek." BATTLE CREEK!!!!! just what I have been waiting for. I would get my prized package and take off running home, ripping the package open as I ran.

When I got home, there it was… A Wild Bill Hickok jack knife. For only two box tops from Kellogg's Sugar Corn Pops (now called Corn Pops), I had a knife to carry to school to show to my second-grade friends... instead of my old Barlow knife.

If we could eat enough Sugar Corn Pops, and if I could talk Daddy and Mama into buying them, there were some other things that I would like to have. There was that Sheriff's Badge... that thing would go just fine with my Wild Bill Hickok jack knife... and, oh, one of those membership cards into the Roy Roger's Clean Plate Club would be a good thing to show to the cooks in the lunchroom in the event I needed extra food.

Also, from Quaker Cereals (I believe), you could get a deed for a square inch of land in the Yukon. That would be a perfect place for me to have a hide out. I got that deed and I was so proud of it. Shoot, I didn't even know what a square inch was.

Some of you do not know how important those things were to a little boy who grew up on the so-called wrong side of the tracks. We didn't get things like kids do today, except at Christmas, and on our birthday.

Dad ended up doing pretty well for himself, and we built a new brick home in the so-called "nicest part of town". One thing I learned is that "people are people." There are good and bad ones from all different parts of society. It is not my job to grade them. To this day, I never ask anyone what they do for a living or where they live... I will just love them for who they are.

My life has been greatly enriched by having friends from all walks of life. bob

SUMMER CIRCA 1955

"Summertime... and the living is easy. Catfish a jumpin' and the cotton is high."

That old George Gershwin song always made me feel at peace with the world. I loved that old song when I was a young child and it still brings me peace. When I think of that song, those idyllic days of summers from long ago come to mind. Let me regress a little for you.

We kids could not wait for summer vacation from school. In those days school ended in late May and reopened September 1st. That gave us three whole months to learn to live, learn, love, and enjoy just being a kid... pretty much on our own terms.

The first event of summer was Vacation Bible School at First Baptist Church in Newton. In those days Bible School started at 9AM and ended at noon and lasted two weeks. With our parents at work, most of us kids looked after ourselves during the day. (I guess that would be called child neglect these days). We would get dressed, prepare our breakfast, and off to Bible School we would go. The first two hours of Bible School consisted of singing and Bible Study and the last hour was craft time... I still have a shoe shine box that I made. We enjoyed the walk to and fro with no adult supervision. Heaven forbid a child walking to town alone these days.

When Bible School ended, it was blackberry picking time. My Aunt Mildred and Uncle Slim who worked 2nd shift jobs would come and get me and take me to a "blackberry bog" near where I live now. I would pick a gallon a day. Mom would can them and make blackberry pies all winter long. I would give anything for a piece of mama's blackberry pie. Nobody could make a blackberry pie like mom... (tearing up a little.)

Of course, there were those Little League baseball games every Tuesday and Thursday. I was so proud of my Prestige uniform

#11. Our coach, and my cousin Steve Sims, would give us cokes or watermelon after each game. What a memory…

In the evenings, I would go to the large, wooden stadium, now demolished, and watch our Class D Newton Conover Twins or American Legion Post 16 play baseball. I can still remember the aroma of hot dogs and popcorn wafting through the air. I rarely had any money for admission, but that was not a problem. I knew a place on the third base side of the field where I could climb the side of the stadium and would end up in the stands. I hope the statute of limitations has run out on that.

Some evenings were spent fishing, playing in someone's yard or riding bicycles. I did not have a bicycle at the time, but I would ride my sister's girls bicycle. I got kidded a lot about that… Shoot, I was just glad to have something to ride.

Dad tried to teach us a work ethic at that early age. I had to hoe and pick the vegetables in the garden. I did not mind the work except picking the okra. The okra made me itch, but I did it anyway. It wouldn't have been so bad if I were decently dressed. My standard dress each day was shorts… yep shorts… just shorts. I thought I looked like Tarzan. I never wore a shirt or shoes all summer long, except to go to church. I also had to mow the yard once a week. That old reel type, no motor, lawn mower was quite difficult for an 8-year old to push.

In mid-August we had the Old Soldiers Reunion. The Old Soldiers Reunion was a time to honor our brave men and women who had served in the military. "Reunion Week" culminated with a large parade and a carnival. The parade was held on Thursday morning, and believe it or not, the cotton mills and furniture factories would close for the day to enable their employees to enjoy the parade with their families. After the parade, we would walk (we didn't have a car) to North Newton to enjoy the carnival which was a big part of the celebration. I could ride one ride and have my choice of a snow cone or cotton candy… man, what a hard decision.

After Old Soldiers Reunion, it was almost September 1st… time to go back to school. The only thing left to look forward too was the World Series which was played in early September… well, it would not be long until Halloween… Beautiful memories from a kid who was…. and well, still is a dreamer. bob

A NICE OLD COUPLE

As we turned into their driveway, I told Gaye that "I believe we are going to meet someone really genuine and special today." You could barely see them through the dust on their golf cart window that they had backed into the carport. In front of the golf cart was a table full of tomatoes, cantaloupes, and watermelons. (I will come back to this in a minute.)

Gaye and I went to the apple house this morning to buy peaches. For those of you who do not live around here, I won't try to explain why you go to an APPLE house to buy PEACHES. On the way to the apple house I saw a handwritten sign in a yard that said, "Cantaloupes/Tomatoes." We decided we needed to stop there on our way back home. Our early tomatoes are over and our late tomatoes are not quite ready yet… and we can always use a cantaloupe.

He stayed in the golf cart until I approached him and introduced myself to him and his bride, who was sitting beside him. He was ONLY 86 and I 'spect his wife was about the same. I thought it would be wise not to ask her.

You could just tell by looking at them that they are the real deal. Folks who had worked all their lives and still working selling their produce. Honest, decent, upstanding... do the right thing, kind of people.

"Tomatoes - six for a dollar and watermelons and cantaloupes $2 each," he told me. I told him that was more than fair. We got 6 tomatoes and one watermelon for $3. I gave him a $5 bill hoping that he did not have change. I started to tell him to keep the change, but I didn't know his American and personal pride would not have allowed for such a thing.

His parting words were, "back around that tree there in the yard... I don't want you backing out onto that highway and getting hit... I don't want to have to call an ambulance for you."

Thank you, Sir for making my day. You brought joy into my life by just being you.

After that we stopped at the grocery store. A very "handsome" young lady of about 35 or so gave me the prettiest smile and greeting you have ever seen. I thanked her for that. She told me that she was full of joy in her heart. That reminded me, and all of y'all remember this, "You can always have joy even if you are not happy." Some of you will understand that.

All it takes is a smile and a pleasant greeting to change someone's day. bob

THE AMERICAN DREAM

I know a young Russian couple who came to America 2 or 3 years ago, seeking the American Dream.

One of Russian's friends Smart Phone broke. AT&T told her that it would cost $150 to fix it. The Russian told her that he would fix it for her. He fixed it for her with a $1.69 part. In the meantime, he started buying used phones, fixing them up and selling them by the case worldwide. It was just an idea that he pursued diligently.

He then bought a semitruck, and an automotive hauler and began hauling cars nationwide. He didn't want to be a truck driver, he wanted to own a trucking company. He has now hired someone to drive his truck and is looking for another truck.

They have moved to Matthews, NC where they bought a townhouse. They are also involved in another business venture. My best bet is that they will be very wealthy in a few years.

They did everything right. They applied for American citizenship, got social security numbers, drivers licenses, including a CDL. They have achieved the American Dream and are loving and appreciating their life in America.

The American Dream... what is it? It is more than having a lot of money, being a member of the country club, or being a well-known person in the community. It is different for all of us.

I achieved the American Dream. My dream was just to live a simple life, live comfortably, and have a nice wife, son, and lots of friends. Those are the things that are important to me. Yes, that sounds simplistic, but it took a lot of hard work.

Some people say that the American Dream is out of reach... hogwash. In the United States of America, we have the freedom to achieve our goals. It could be as simple as mine or as complex as owning a railroad. Whatever....it is still in reach.

It is ironic to me that the Russian couple have already achieved the American Dream....and they are not Americans yet. They simply worked hard and overcame whatever was in their way. When I went to Vietnam the first time, they told us that when things go wrong.... adapt and adjust.

I am thinking that Colonel Sanders was around sixty when he opened his first KFC. You are never too young or too old.

Hopefully, some of you are encouraged by my random thoughts today. bob

KILLING HOGS

When I went to check on the cows this morning, I made a big mistake. Wearing shorts and a T shirt and riding on an ATV was not a good idea on this chilly morning. I like to froze to death. It reminded me of Fall years ago...

Back in the 70's, Billy Little and I would each buy a pig every year. When I bought our farm, there was a pig pen on the place so it made sense that I would raise them. Billy and I would both feed them until late fall when it was time for the slaughter.

Billy had a very nice meat processing building where we would slaughter them. Although that processing building was only for Billy's personal use, it was as well-equipped as any professional processing plant that I have ever been in.

We all had our jobs. My job was to salt, sugar, season and wrap the hams to be hung in one of my outbuildings until spring when they would be fully cured. My other job was to grind the sausage and season it with my own special blend of herbs and spices.

Billy's job was to slaughter the hogs and slice up the tenderloins, pork chops etc.

Billy's mother-in-law, Kat, was always present to make the liver mush. That was appreciated, but it was not the most important thing she did. She would bake biscuits and fry tenderloin and sausage for us....and our friends

Every one of our friends would come to this affair to eat fresh pork and biscuits...I don't remember if we invited them or if they just showed up... I 'spect it was the latter. This would go on until about midnight when everyone went home with a full belly...

It really was not a night of meat cutting... it was a night of friendship. All of those old friends are gone now. I am the only one left. I have new friends now, but I can't forget those memories of long ago. It was quite a party. bob

THE HAIRCUT

"What in the world happened to your hair????" Those were Gaye's words as I entered the house. Well....let me explain...

Crystal Barnes Pearson has cut my hair for at least 15 years. She is always good to work me into her schedule to meet any of my "emergencies." I was overdue and needed my hair cut today due to our weekend schedule. Crystal was booked for the day, but she offered to cut it after closing. That was not fair to her and I would not allow that. Crystal and I talked it over and we agreed that I would have to let someone else cut it. Dang, I hated that. It was my fault for not planning ahead.

I decided to go to one of those places with a fancy-sounding French name. I figured that they would have someone from Paris especially trained in daintily clipping tresses such as mine… I envisioned myself walking proudly and tall, resembling a movie star after they got through with me.

I strolled into this fancy place and asked If they accepted "walk ins." They said they had a girl in the back who could cut it immediately. "OK", I said, as they went to get her.

I was just standing there and was beginning to get a little nervous about why they kept her in the backroom… and then it happened. She sauntered out, looked me up and town, and firmly proclaimed, "So, whadda ya want!!!!! A haircut?" I was immediately frightened and intimidated. "Yes ma'am," I meekly replied…"Well, sit down then," she boomed.

Fear and anxiety was overcoming my body, but I did as she said. "Do you like it cut with scissors or shears?" I told her that I prefer scissors because that is how Crystal does it. She said, I can do just as well with shears as she turned them on. She grabbed a handful of hair nearly jerking me out of my seat… I vaguely heard my neck pop as my scalp stretched inches away from my skull…

She continued to grab fistfuls of hair and jerk me around. In just about 5 minutes she was through. My scalp, neck, and even my hair hurt. As she pulled my hair one last time she asked, "How does that suit you?" In fear of reprisal or maybe even death, I told her it was just wonderful. I sure did not want to make her angry.

As I limped out the door, looking back to make sure she wasn't stalking me, I began to feel better. I have lived through mortar and rocket attacks, small arms fire, and a date with 'that' girl from Morganton… and now this. I feel sure God is setting me up and using all these things to make me stronger. I know He is not through with me yet.

Please do not worry about me. I will probably be fine after a little bedrest and a few more Aleve. Thank God for Crystal Pearson. bob

KEEP YOUR FINGERS OUT OF MY MOUTH

Gaye and I stopped at our favorite Subway on the way home from the Y. When we first got there, only one person was working… making the sandwiches and operating the cash register. After a minute or two, a lady came out from the back to help. I am thinking that she had probably been to the bathroom.

Before taking her place behind the counter, she washed her hands, pushed her hair back with her hands, put a rubber band around her pony tail, and began work. I don't know the sanitary rules at restaurants, but I think she did it backwards.

… and it gets worse.

Gaye and I were sitting in a booth eating our sandwiches. The couple in the booth behind us stood up to leave. They were a very nice-looking, sophisticated couple, probably in their early 60's. As the lady stood up, her arm lightly grazed my neck or shoulder. She apologized and I turned back towards her to accept her apology. I had just taken a bite of my sandwich and was in the process of wiping my mouth when this happened. The lady said, "wait a minute," and before I had a chance to ask her what to wait a minute for, she stuck her fingers in the corner of my mouth and got that little piece of lettuce that I was getting ready to wipe. Gaye's mouth was hanging agape and I was speechless… and then…

The husband said to his wife, "Are you cavorting with another man?" She replied, "Yes, right in front of his wife." We exchanged a few other pleasantries and they left.

She would have stood a whole lot better chance if she would keep her fingers out of my mouth. bob

HONKEY TONKS

Well, Gaye is out of town on a little excursion with a few girl-friends. I guess that means that I can play today. I think I will go to a Honky Tonk. Yep, that's exactly what I'll do.

Do any of you even know what a Honky Tonk is?... I doubt it. Let me give you a brief history of Honky Tonks.

Back in the 1930's it was not common for people to date those of other races. When a white guy dated a black girl, he would never go to the door to get her in fear of being beat up. He would just sit in his car and "honk" his horn for his date to come out... hence the word "Honky."

They would often go to a cheap, tiny, non-descript bar that accepted mixed couples on their date. Most of these bars had a cheap piano named a Tonk. (You can google Tonk pianos and learn all about them.) The bars soon became known as Honky Tonks.

Now where did the term Honky Tonk Music come from? During that era most of the black girls liked jazz and blues. The white guys liked "hillbilly." Soon the musicians at the honky tonk combined the jazz, blues, and hillbilly and formed a new genre of music called Honky Tonk. Therefore, "honky tonk" referred to a type of music as well as the building.

That is your history lesson for today. No, I am not going to a Honky Tonk. I am thinking of going to a Methodist Church chicken dumpling/chicken pie fundraiser that I read about in the paper… life in the fast lane. bob

EATING AT MATTIE'S

Gaye and I stopped at a little café for lunch today. In the 70's and 80's that café was a meeting place for local farmers. We almost always had breakfast there while solving the world's problems… I went back to memory lane today.

Here are a few examples of some adventures that I enjoyed while eating there around 40 years ago:

One morning I arrived and joined the guys at the big table where we always ate. The big table was sort of a community table that seated about 10 or 12 people. They had a new waitress that morning who did not know me. I decided to have a little fun with her.

When she asked me what I wanted I replied, "I believe I will have the eggs benedict." Eggs benedict was not on the menu and no one in there even knew what eggs benedict was… including me. When Mattie, the owner of the café, saw my order she said, "Who in the @@@@ ordered that? The waitress pointed at me. Mattie said, "I might have known it woulda been him." A couple minutes later the waitress brought me a bowl of pintos smothered with onions. Mattie kept peeping around the corner and grinning as she watched me eat those pintos for breakfast. As I was leaving, I thanked Mattie for the free breakfast and walked out the door. I never did pay for them. Mattie and I laughed about that for years.

One day we were sitting in there and, lo and behold, in came two guys leading two horses... Yes, you read correctly, they brought horses into the restaurant. Mattie came running from the back and yelled, "Git those horses outta here!!!!" They replied, "It's your fault... you don't have a hitching post outside... there is nowhere to park them." It did not take long to get those horses out.

One afternoon I stopped in for something cool to drink. I was sitting at the counter beside of a man that I did not know... He was a stranger passing through who stopped for a hamburger and a beer. Mattie looked from the back and saw me sitting there with that guy and she gave me the finger. The man, a somewhat sophisticated looking fellow asked, "What did she do that for?" Of course, she was giving me the finger just for fun, but I told the man...."She doesn't like strangers and she usually gives them the finger." I never did tell him the truth.

All I can say is Mattie loved us and we loved Mattie. She is long gone now, but she championed each and every one of us. She had our backs... Man, if the walls in that building could talk.... bob

GOOD MEMORIES

I was talking to my 40-year old son who lives in Charlotte on the telephone Sunday night. We were talking about the World Series. He asked me if I remembered taking him to Tommy Sigmon's Store when he was very young and buying hot dogs to eat while we watched the World Series on TV. He said that we came home and watched the game on a small TV in the bedroom. What a beautiful memory.

Last night at Trunk or Treat at our church, I was talking to a 59-year old man that I taught in Sunday School when he was 13. He still remembered something that I talked about. He then said that he did not have a good home life with his dad and that "you were my mentor." That caused my eyes to spring a leak.

All of this tells me that you need to be careful what you say and do. You never know when a very impressionable young boy or girl is watching. I have failed so many times.

Sometimes a blind squirrel can find an acorn and sometimes an old, unsophisticated country boy does something right. bob

HIGH SCHOOL KIDS

This post goes back to the mid 90's when our son, Justin, was in high school.

Our house was a hangout for the boys and girls in Justin's class. We almost always had a house full. Here are a few stories that happened over 20 years ago:

We never had a set curfew for Justin. His curfew depended on what he was doing and where he was going. We had a rule that if he was going to be late that he should give us a call prior to the time he was scheduled to be home and we would make other arrangements.

One night, Justin said he was going to go to Eric's after the Friday night football game to play video games. He said he would be home at midnight. At about 11:55PM he called and said that he was going to be late because they had not even started playing yet. Fine, we understood. About 5 minutes later we saw some car lights shining through our bedroom window as it rounded the curve in the driveway. We wondered why Justin had decided to come home... probably to get some video games and then go back to Eric's. About 10 minutes later, an odor was wafting throughout the house. I thought the septic tank was backing up. I got up to see what was going on. There was a fellow named Josh on the sofa all covered up with a blanket, watching TV, and eating a microwave pizza that he got out of the freezer and nuked. Those kids felt at home here. We treated them as family and they treated us with the respect that you show to an elder.

We often would get phone calls from their parents offering to pay us or send food for all those kids. That was never a problem. If we happened to run out of snack food and drinks, they would eat whatever they could find... beanie weenies, cereal, canned pineapple, eggs... in other words... anything. One night they had run out of snacks and were eating cereal. A late comer from another high school showed up and they told him that they were eating cereal. They handed him a little individual serving packet and told him it was Fruity Pebbles. They never did tell him that it was actually a pack of cat food that looked like Fruity Pebbles. I do not remember how that story ended.

In those days, cable had not reached this part of the county. Most people just had an antenna. I invested in a great big, probably 6-foot, satellite dish. The kids loved that thing. They would often come over to watch sporting events on ESPN. One night they were coming over to watch a hockey game. I think the game started at 8pm, but not sure. Gaye and I both had meetings and Justin was at Karate class. I was the first one home, and the driveway was full of cars. I entered the house and there sat about a dozen boys drinking soft drinks and eating popcorn. I spoke to them and walked to another part of the house. When I walked back to the den one of them said, "Mr. Marlowe, have you noticed that no one from your family is here?" Well, no, I hadn't noticed. They had become part of the family.

One night two brothers were on the way over here. The phone rang and they asked to speak to Justin, but he wasn't home yet. When they found out Justin wasn't home, one asked, "Mr. Marlowe, do you know how to change a tire?" They told me where they were and I went and showed them how to change a tire. I didn't do it for them. Like I said, we treated them as family. They needed to learn to change a tire, not have it done for them. A couple days later they came over here and gave me a James Taylor CD. That is just the way those kids were.

I think about those kids from time to time. I try to remember each and every one of them. The ones that I remember have all done well for themselves and are strewn all over the country. They were good young 'uns. bob

THE BENEDICTION

I was honored and delighted to be invited to speak to the Golden Age Club this morning. It was a great time with some old friends. In fact, I wouldn't mind being a member If I were old enough.

I asked them what their favorite part of the worship service was. They said things like music, Bible readings, sermon, etc.... the usual things.

Of course, I prefer to be different and surprised everyone when I told them that my favorite part is the Benediction. It got quite a laugh. When you hear the Benediction, that means it is time to put on your jacket, wipe the sleep from your eyes, and rush to the cafeteria to try to beat the Baptists and Methodists.

Actually...

The Benediction is a blessing that you take with you and remember all week. It will give you strength and courage as you go through your occasional difficult days... and now,

The Lord Bless You and Keep You.
The Lord Make His Face to Shine Upon You and be Gracious to You.
The Lord Lift Up His Countenance Upon You and Give You Peace. bob

SUMMER 1958

I believe that the summer of 1958 was the favorite summer of my youth.

We moved to South Newton, to the new house that Daddy had built. That was also the first year that South Newton Elementary School was in operation. Another thing that made that summer special was all the new friends I made. There were kids of my age group everywhere. My best friends were the Thornburg boys, Eddie and Steve, and Al Kale, Ben Huss, Dudley Locke, and Johnny Hunsucker. They lived within a block of me and we played outside from morning until after dark.

Just a few blocks from where we lived was a well-stocked fish pond. The owner was a nice man who always allowed us to fish anytime. Adjacent to the fish pond was a business called Cline's Floats. They were, I believe, the largest float manufacturer in the United States. I remember that they sent floats to the Rose Bowl Parade one year. There was a big field beside of Cline's Floats that they used as a parking lot for several World War II Army

Jeeps. They used the Jeeps to pull the floats to various destinations throughout the United States.

When we got tired of fishing, we would get into those Jeeps and drive them around in the large field. We did not have permission, but Mr. Cline knew that we did it... well, we sorta had permission.

One day David Sims and I were fishing. When we got through fishing David wanted to walk to town to get a Reese's Cup and a cherry Pepsi at Smith Drug Store. He had a dime and it was burning up his pocket. I said, "I will drive us to town if you will share the cherry Pepsi and Reese's Cup with me." I didn't have any money so he agreed.

We got in one of those Jeeps and my 12-year old self drove us to town. We got our snack, and on the way back home, a Newton policeman by the name of Ivy Hass stopped me. Being a small town where everyone knew everyone, Officer Hass recognized me. He stopped me because the Jeep did not have a license plate... not because I was 12 years old and driving without a license in a "stolen" car. He told me to take the Jeep back to Clines and he would meet me there and take me home.

When we got to Clines, Mr. Cline met us in the parking lot. He was very nice and told us not to get on the road again with that Jeep. Officer Hass put David and me in the police car and drove us home.

By the time we got to my house, Mr. Cline had already called my dad and told him that everything was fine and not to be too hard on me. Officer Hass told the whole story to my dad and everyone ended up laughing about it.

It was a kinder and gentler time. bob

MY NEW SUIT

Well, my reputation has spread to a clothing company that I have never heard of.

I got an email today telling me that I needed to buy some of their clothes because I need to improve my "professional image." Shoot, I didn't even know that I had a professional image... good or bad.

I have a closet full of shirts and trousers with the tags still on them... mostly gifts. I just prefer to wear the same old five or six shirts and pants over and over. Some are probably 10 or 15 years old........ I do buy a lot of underwear though.

Just this moment, Gaye walked in here with a Duluth Trading Company jacket that I got for Christmas a few years ago... still has the tags on it. I didn't even know that I had it. I rekon' I should wear it, but I am partial to a Dollar General flannel sweater type jacket that a good friend brought me six or seven years ago when he came down here from the mountains to deer hunt.

I have a problem in my way of thinking about clothes, I guess. I do not notice what other people wear. Luckily, I have reached a point in life where I notice the inner beauty of folks rather than their outer beauty and clothing. Apparently, most people are superficial and look at the pretty, shiny, exterior instead of the more important heart. Here is a good example:

When my son got married, I did not own a suit. I never wear a suit. I quit wearing them over 20 years ago. Luckily, when you get to my age, you can wear just about anything... anytime or anywhere and get by with it. I wanted to wear a nice suit to my son's wedding so I went to a high-dollar men's store to buy a complete outfit. When the salesman finally came to wait on me, she looked me up and down and said… "and just what is your budget?" I should have exited the store, but I assured her that I could afford any suit in the store and could probably buy every suit they had if I so desired. I spent a heap of money that day… I don't remember the total price, but the tie was over $100. I would have probably looked just as good if I had bought the things at Penny's or Sear's.

Anyway, I don't spect' I will respond to the email about improving my professional image. I am going to stay the same. Oh, by the way, I do get a haircut often, take a bath and shave every day and my old clothes are always clean… at least when I put 'em on. I ain't changing. bob

VACCINES

There is a lot of talk going around about flu shots. Many praise them, and many say, "No, No, No." Here is my assessment:

There is a religious community in our area who do not go to doctors or take modern medicine except on very rare occasions… One of the members, a grown man, said that he has only been to the doctor once in his life… for a broken arm. These folks obviously do not take the flu shot.

They operate a very nice and very popular restaurant in our area. In addition to their restaurant, they raise their own food, drink goat milk, and farm. They do not drink, smoke, or eat pork. I have become friends with many of these people and I love every one of them. Their lifestyle is different from mine, but they are fine people… the kind of people I like to call friend.

One of my friends was talking to them at the restaurant. He asked how many people in their community has had the flu this season. The answer is NONE.

You would think, and I am positively sure, that they came in contact with the flu virus from the many customers in the restaurant… then, logically, they would pass it on to other members of their community who do not work in the restaurant. (They live together in houses adjacent to their restaurant.)

All I can say is they work hard, eat properly (they all look healthy), have healthy lifestyles, and keep clean. You can draw from this story whatever you want to if anything. I am just telling the story. bob

BLUE PLATE

I caved one day this past week… so ashamed of myself.

With the closing of **BI-LO** and Honey's Supermarkets, I haven't been able to find a supplier of Blue Plate Mayo. Gaye brought home a jar of that nasty Dukes stuff. It was so bad that I would not even put it on a BLT. I had to find Blue Plate.

I found it on the internet… $8 a jar. I was tempted to order it at that high price. Gaye, who is a better and smarter shopper than me, found out that the Walmart Hometown Market in Newton has it. I said I would rather pay the higher price on the internet than to enter that place. I don't mind regular Walmarts, but it is against everything I believe in to go in one of those neighborhood store things… every time one of those Walmart Hometown Markets open, the local stores go out of business.

We were riding through Newton this past Thursday and Gaye said, "Let's stop at that Walmart thing and get some Blue Plate." No ma'am," I sternly replied, "I ain't going into that place." With my reputation about those Walmart Grocery things, it would have been worse than a Baptist getting caught in the liquor store.

I caved… but I didn't go in though. Gaye went in and got a couple of jars of Blue Plate. While she was inside the store, I stayed in the car, sitting down in the seat, with an oversized hat pulled low on my head. I do not think anyone saw me.

Well, at least I am happy now. bob

FULL CIRCLE

Most of the time things go full circle.

When I was a teenager and even younger, I loved to listen to my 45 RPM single records and 33 1/3 albums on my record player. In the 70's, here come the 8 track tapes. I never did like those things, but I bought a few of them, but still stuck to my record albums. It wasn't long until cassette tapes came on the scene. I liked them a little better than 8 tracks… but not much better. The next thing was the Compact Disc. I liked them for their clarity and sound, but still bought my vinyl albums when I could. It wasn't long until I could no longer get vinyl albums… everything went to CD.

Now some artists do not even put out CD's anymore… you have to buy it digitally online. Well, I don't particularly care for most of the new artists anyway, and there is no way I am going to walk around, looking stupid and anti-social, with those ear bud things stuck in my ears… or whatever you call them.

I love music and really miss my old ways of listening to music. One day I was in Circuit City… and lo and behold… there was a record player for sale. I was so excited with the record player that I forgot to buy whatever it was I went in there for. My heart started beating out of my chest and slobber was running down my chin. It had been years since I had seen a record player. I had to have it. I could not wait to get through the check-out line and get home to play some of my old music. I then started ordering "old timey" music on vinyl from the Ernest Tubb Record Shop in Nashville, some dating back to the 30's. With all of those albums and my old collection, I was in hog heaven.

I heard on the radio this morning that more and more artists are beginning to make vinyl available to us old timers. The millennials will probably think it is something new. Yep, everything goes full circle.

Sometimes when things go full circle, it is a time of renewal. I have been working on the fence line all day...a beautiful day here in North Carolina, about 80 degrees. I enjoyed looking at the Spring flowers already blooming and the maple trees are beginning to show signs of their red buds. I stopped by our pond as I was riding my ATV to where I had parked the truck. Oh, it was wonderful to see the bass swimming in the shallows on the sunny side of the pond. After a hard winter, these are beautiful sights to me... things are going full circle.

Spring is a time of renewal of my old self... after all, the seasons have gone full circle.... so maybe that is a sign that I need to do so myself. That is my way of looking at it anyway. Maybe you might want to do to your own self. I have a long way to go, and a lot of renewing to do, but I'm gonna work on it. Maybe I can go full circle back to those wonderful days of the 50's and 60's. bob

THE WONDER BRA

Several years ago, Gaye met a lady named Louise at a shower or some such thing. Louise had recently lost her husband and was naturally lonely and afraid. She had no close friends, just acquaintances, and her family lived away from here. Gaye, as only her sweet and kind self knows how to do, offered to help her if she ever needed anything.

From time to time, Louise would call Gaye to take her places like the grocery store or to a doctor's appointment. Louise drove and had a car... I just think that she sometimes just needed someone to cater to her and buy her lunch.

Louise called one day and asked if Gaye would come over and till a small space in her garden and to mow her back yard. She had a tiller and mower, but she was not sure they would crank. Gaye took me along to help.

When we arrived at her house, Louise was getting ready to go somewhere and said she would be back in an hour or so. I soon got the tiller started and Gaye began tilling and setting out tomato plants. It wasn't long until I got the mower running and was mowing the back yard.

Like many country women, Louise would hang her clothes on the clothesline if the weather permitted. Here is where things went from bad to worse. As I was trying to mow under that clothesline, I somehow knocked a bra off onto the ground. Before I could get stopped, the bra got caught in the lawnmower blades. That bra went from a 38 to a 30 in a matter of two seconds. Pieces of that bra were everywhere.

At about that time, Gaye had finished up her tilling and was walking to where I was. "What are we going to do," I asked? Gaye said it looks like an old bra and Louise would probably not care. I said, "No, I am going to buy her a new bra." I thought that it might be embarrassing for Louise and I did not want her to know. We looked at all the pieces of that bra and found the tag. I took off to the nearest store, Kmart, while Gaye finished mowing the back yard. It did not take me long to find a bra with the same numbers....in fact it was the same brand and everything... I was lucky.

I got back to the house and Gaye had finished mowing and was putting the lawn mower away. I tore the price tag and other labels off that bra and hung in on the line at the exact same place... just as Louise was returning home.

Louise, a church woman, rarely cussed but she would from time to time for emphasis. "What in the hell is that on my line," she asked? "Huh," I innocently answered. She took off to the clothesline at breakneck speed for a woman of her age and said she did not have any bras that new. I tried to explain to her that the sunshine would bring out the freshness in things....it does for our sheets anyway. She was looking confused and we left.

Yep, I highly recommend those solar dryers to refurbish your old bras. You can thank me later. bob

KRISPY KREME "HOT LIGHT" SPECIAL

On the way home from getting my truck serviced, I noticed that the Krispy Kreme "Hot" light was on.......well, it wasn't exactly like that...... I have a personal policy not to go to the KK unless the hot light is on.......Today was one of those days that I had to drive around in the area for 1 1/2 hours waiting for it to come on.

I ordered a coffee and doughnuts at the drive through window. When I got to the window to pick up my order, one of the most wholesome and sweet looking girls with the most pleasant smile I had ever seen took my payment. She came back and gave me the coin change and explained that they were changing shifts, and I would have to wait for $3 in bills.

It was taking longer than expected. She came to the window and apologized and asked if she could give me an extra doughnut for having to wait so long. "I'll tell you what," I replied, "you can give me an extra doughnut if you want to, but you will have to keep the $3 for yourself if you will keep smiling."… Well, she gave me two extra free doughnuts… As I drove away everyone was happy.

I think the happiest one of the bunch was Gaye when I got home and told her, "I stopped at Krispy Kreme and got you two doughnuts." Notice I said "got" not "bought."

It is cold, dreary, and rainy here today, but that smiling lass brightened my day. I hope we all follow her example. Shoot, there ain't no reason not to. bob

MISS MARGARET'S STORE

It doesn't look like much, but it was one of my favorite places to go.

The roof has fallen in on the left side of the building. The inside is old and rustic. When the business started 65 years ago, it was a true general store. They had everything from hardware to food. It has changed over the years.

The owners still sell a few groceries, but the main business is ice cream… cones, cups, and milkshake… probably the best milk-shakes on Planet Earth. It was also a good place to get a cold cut sandwich. Miss Margaret would slice bologna, ham, lunch meat, and cheese from a big roll. It went good in any combination… sliced thick on Sunbeam bread with mayo and mustard. You just can't get that anywhere. I could get a bologna and cheese sandwich, a cone of ice cream, and a canned grape drink for $2.75... a meal fit for a king.

Miss Margaret, the owner, was one of my favorite people. With the advent of Dollar General Stores and Walmart, the old store loved by many of us had to close this week. That is a sad state of affairs.

I have been sad since I heard of their closing early this week. I sure will miss Miss Margaret. They don't make them like her anymore. It hurts to see a landmark of the community have to close. Bowman's Grocery was the best. The Whittenburg Community will never be the same. Shop locally. bob

EATING DOG FOOD

My doctor, Robert Glenn Auton Jr, works with me quite a bit about trying to lose twenty or so pounds. This past month I have been on a low carb and low sugar diet. I look forward to weighing in Thursday morning at my follow up appointment... something I usually dread.

I have really been doing well. In fact, I am proud of myself. I haven't cheated a bit and Gaye says the diet is working.

Friday night I saw a baggie full of little cookies on the kitchen table. They were about as around as a quarter and maybe a 1/4 inch thick. I decided to cheat a little bit and eat a couple.

I poured a 1/2 glass of milk and held one of the cookies in the milk until it stopped bubbling (to make sure it was saturated good) and ate it. It was not sweet at all...in fact it had no taste. I ate one more and decided that was enough.

Yesterday, I saw Gaye feeding one of them to one of our dogs. I told her that they were not fit for human consumption and to give them all to the dogs. She said, "You haven't been eating those dog snacks, have you?"…"Well, yeah, I ate two of them."

It seems that someone had given them to Gaye's sister because her dog would not eat them. Then Gaye's sister gave them to Gaye because her dog wouldn't eat them.

Well, Robert, when I show up for my appointment Thursday morning, please check me out for worms, parvo, fleas, and heart worms… and my rabies shot is overdue.

AARF. AARF. bob

PERCEPTIONS OF OURSELVES

Sometimes we perceive things about ourselves differently than other people. Maybe you think that new outfit or suit you just bought looks good on you… there are those who will disagree. We all have different perceptions about the same thing.

About 35 or so years ago, the administrator of the place that I worked went on a business trip to Dallas. He was gone for about a week. This 60ish man was very short and well… fat… he was about as wide as he was tall.

The day that he returned from his business trip he joined me at my table in the company cafeteria for lunch. Good Lord, I have never seen such a change in a man……in only one week.

Not only had his voice and attitude changed, but his appearance had changed as well. He was wearing a cowboy hat, a string tie, and cowboy boots. Good gracious, he didn't look like a cowboy to me.

"Bob, did you know that the oilmen and cowboys in Texas leave their hat on while they eat in restaurants," he asked. "I have seen it on TV… I just didn't know if it was really like that or not," I replied.

"Who do you think I look like," was his next question. "Well, I just don't know," I answered. "Here is a hint for you... this person is on TV every Friday night." After I little thought I answered, "Boss Hog on the Dukes of Hazard."

He looked perplexed and said he was thinking he looked like J. R. Ewing on Dallas. Thinking quickly, I told him that "I always thought Boss Hog and J. R. Ewing look exactly alike."

He quit wearing his hat, boots, and tie after that episode... and I don't think I got a raise that year... and yeah, J. R and Boss Hog look exactly alike. You bet. bob

WIND CHIMES

Gaye is happy with the smallest of things.

She went to a fundraiser Saturday night. Every person at her table had a gift waiting at their seat. Gaye got a small basil plant. She was thrilled with it. You would have thought someone gave her million dollars.

When she got home, I was already in bed. She came to the bedroom to show me all of the items she got at the silent auction... but she was most proud of this little plant.

One day last week she went with me to a co-op store. She particularly likes this store because they have a "home" department. She always picks up some little item.

Last week she didn't see anything she wanted. I told her to get one of those sets of chimes that I thought were pretty. I was roaming around the store when Gaye found me and asked me if I wanted the chimes in the key of A, D, G, or C. I told her C is always a good key to play in. She wasn't paying any attention to the price and neither was I. I thought they were probably about $19.95.

I bought about $70 worth of stuff. When I went to the counter to pay my bill… It was $200. Those dang chimes cost $129.95. I did not say anything about the high price. She is worth it, and after all, they were made in the good old USA.

I am glad that I bought those things. I thought that they would just jingle, but they sound like the pipe organ at the Mormon Tabernacle. I have never heard anything like it. Well worth the price. She deserves it. bob

MY TOWN

Small towns are the best… Period.

Yesterday a tick bite that I received a day or two, prior was still swollen and sore. Without an appointment I went to my doctor's office in my hometown of Newton, NC to see if they could work me in. I got there around 8AM and his first appointment is at 8:15AM. He saw me sitting in the lobby and I told him what was going on. He took me into his office, checked it out, and told me how to treat it before his 8:15AM appointment. Also, he said to have Gaye keep check on it. I was only in there for about 5 minutes from the time I entered the building until I returned to my car. Not many doctors would do that. Dr. Robert Glenn Auton is the best. That is small town living.

When I left there, I went to a café on the town square for breakfast. I sat down in a booth, and the first thing I saw was the "community table." That is the table for good old boys to sit and talk about their day, tell their stories, and then go home, to work, or another hangout. My best bet is that most of them are there every day. There were blue/white collar, professionals, and retirees. As soon as someone would leave, another would enter and take the empty seat. I feel sure that is their daily routine. When they tell their last story, most likely they start at the beginning and begin anew. Southern living at its best.

My waitress called me "Hon" and the waitress that filled my coffee cup called me "Sug." It was not a term of endearment or a way of flirting… that is what southern girls do… just small-town southern living.

When I left the café, I looked around the courthouse square and everything looked pretty much as it did 50 years ago. The same buildings… just different stores.

As I looked around the square, I thought of the stores that were there in the 50's and 60's that I loved so much. There was Moretz Department Store, Smith's Drug Store, Abernethy Hardware, Clines 5 and Dime, Rexall Drug Store, The Young Men's Shop, Eagles 5 and Dime, Belk's Department Store, Newton Furniture Store, Rhyne's Hardware, Sanitary Grocery, Zollie Howard's Hardware, Moose's Hardware, Oxenford's, and the City Pharmacy. They are gone now and are greatly missed by those from my generation. I wish that the children growing up in Newton today could enjoy the magical fantasies that most of the kids felt back in the day when we entered those stores.

On the Southwest side of the square is a new monument that is only 10 or 15 years old. I guess it will always be the "new monument" until another is erected. It lists the names of the heroes from Catawba County, from the Gulf Wars and back to previous wars, who lost their lives in battle. Sitting beside that monument on a bench was an older gentleman… just quietly sitting there. I do not know if he was reflecting or just resting. It would have been nice to talk to him and hear his story, but he didn't need to be disturbed.

When that monument was first erected, I got a call one night from a fellow who wanted me to unveil the monument at Old Soldier's Reunion, a yearly celebration that has been going on for over 100 years. I do not know how I was selected for that honor, but it stands out in my mind as a great memory.

That is enough reminiscing for now. I guess you could say that it is sort of like Mayberry around here. It's my town. You can always go home, but you can never go back. bob

WEDDING ANNIVERSARY

Well, here it is June 20th… our wedding anniversary. It has been 48 great years for me… probably not so much for Gaye, but she hung in there.

In May of 1967 my grandfather died, and I came home on emergency leave from the Navy to attend the funeral.

On the Saturday after the funeral, I was riding around the square in Newton which was what young people did in those days. Gaye was home from college and was also riding around the square with one of her friends.

Anyway, we met and I fell in love immediately. She didn't care much for me. She later told me that I was arrogant and cocky. Well, I guess I was. I was almost through with some of the toughest training that the Navy had to offer… I thought I was invincible. I was scheduled to begin my first of two voluntary tours in Vietnam in July. I asked her if she would write to me while I was over there. She said she would… not because she liked me, but it was the patriotic thing to do.

Vietnam brought me down to size pretty quickly and I guess she could see that I was changing and that the arrogance was leaving me.

I got discharged in March of 69 and we got married in June of 1970. It has been a wonderful 48 years for me.

We don't have much of a celebration planned. We are going to Long Horn for lunch. I bought her a new leather-bound Bible (that I hope comes today). She is going to buy me a new knife. Although I have 250 knives, I lost my favorite one last week. After lunch we are going to some hardware stores and try to find another one like it…

It has been quite a party. bob

YOU CAN TELL A FRIEND

It has been a good day so far. I had my checkup at the doctor and all looked good. I have lost three pounds since last month. I would like to lose about seven more pounds although some people think I look skinny now.

My fine nurse, Kelsey, had a little fun with me today. When she came out to the lobby to get me, she smiled and said, "You have your shirt on wrong side out"… sure enough, I did. Don't ask me how that happened, I do not know unless Gaye put it on the hanger wrong side out which is not likely. It was a red pull-over silk shirt with 3 buttons at the top which looked almost the same inside out or right side out. The only difference was the tag showed when it was wrong side out. It doesn't matter much anyway… I was not the least bit embarrassed. We laughed and had fun with it.

It is important to tell things like that to your friends when you notice it. It is better for you, a friend, instead of a total stranger telling them.

A few years ago, I went to lunch with a fine, cultured lady from a very wealthy family. After we finished lunch, she went to the restroom and I was waiting for her in the lobby of the restaurant.

Oh, my goodness and lo and behold, when she emerged from the rest room there was a stream of toilet paper about 3 feet long, trailing along behind her from underneath her skirt.

I knew that I had to tell her. My mind was working rapidly. I decided it would be best to tell her after we got into her fine Mercedes… I didn't want her pulling on that paper while we were in the parking lot or restaurant lobby. That would have made matters worse.

As we were walking to her car, I walked slightly behind her. Every couple steps (visualize) I would sling my leg sideways and try to step on that trail of toilet paper, but never succeeded. It was probably best that it didn't work. I didn't have any idea what the other end of that toilet paper was stuck to so it was probably best that things worked out as they did.

When I told her, you can imagine how embarrassed she was. She stayed red until we got back to my place of business.

The next time I saw her, she thanked me. It was better coming from me than for her to walk around like that for the rest of the day.

I wish someone would have told me the time I wore a pair of white pants to work. Underneath those pants was a pair of white boxers that had red hearts all over them. Those red hearts were shining right through those white pants for everyone to see. Well, I wondered why everyone laughed when they saw me that day. I didn't know a thing about it until I got home and Gaye told me. That was fine too. No big deal. Always remember my motto, "Don't sweat the small stuff… everything is small stuff." bob

I LOVE RADIO… ALWAYS HAVE

From my earliest childhood years until the present, I have always been fascinated by radio. In fact, to this day I rarely watch TV if there is a radio close by.

As a youngster living with my parents, we did not have a TV, so naturally the radio was king. We would gather around the radio at night and listen to The Lone Ranger, Boston Blackie and others. Sometimes we would just listen to music on the local radio station. My dad would call in and request, "Too Old to Cut the Mustard" by Bill Carlisle and all the Little Carlisle's for our neighbor John. Of course, John was also listening and he would then call in a request for some such song and dedicate it to my dad. It was good-natured fun and it gave everyone something to laugh about the next day. It didn't take much to entertain us.

When it was time for me to go to bed, I would turn on my AM bedside radio (no such thing as FM at the time) and listen to the distant stations such as 650 Nashville, 700 Cincinnati, 750 Atlanta, 840 Louisville, 880 New York, 890 Chicago, 1100 Cleveland, 1510 Nashville, and 1530 Cincinnati. I would listen until I drifted off to dreamland. Mom or Dad would come in some time during the night and turn it off.

When I was in high school, the local radio stations signed off at 11PM with the National Anthem. Most of us would then listen to 890 Chicago to a disc jockey named Dick Bionti (probably spelled wrong). He was way ahead of his time as far as disc jockeys go.

In those days most of the girls we dated had to be home at 11PM. After taking our date home, we guys would meet at the parking lot of the Harris Teeter Store and ride around and terrorize the town. One cold winter night, we got into a friend's convertible and decided to ride with the top down. We were laughing and sharing stories when suddenly a song like we had never heard came on the radio. It was "Please, Please Me" (I think) by the Beatles. The car got quiet as we took in that new type of rock and roll. We later found out that Dick Bionti was the only one playing Beatle music. That was the first time, that the Beatles had ever been played in America. That was the end of "Be Bop Rock 'n roll". The British Invasion had begun... we just didn't know it yet.

I have every kind of radio you can think of... AM/FM, weather, CB, airplane controllers, ham, and shortwave. I still listen to the stations listed above. I particularly enjoy short wave and listening to stations from all around the world.

I was looking at radios today and happened to see a police/fire/emergency scanner. It seemed to me that I needed one of those. Gaye said that it would make a good birthday gift for me so she bought it and gave it to me a week or so early. I have programmed in all of the local police, fire, and sheriff's departments so far. It is very interesting to listen to.

Imagination is the key to listening to the radio. When I am listening to the Grand Ole Opry on WSM 650 Nashville or a sporting event, I can actually see it and feel the excitement.

Yep, I saw it all on my radio. bob

WISE BEYOND HIS YEARS

Sometimes you can learn from a child, you just have to pay attention.

I do not spend change. I use paper currency for everything that I buy. Each night I put all of the change that I have accumulated that day in a Maxwell House coffee container. It is usually about 3/4 full after about six months. I then take it to the machine at

Walmart that counts your change. The machine gives you a receipt, you take the receipt to the customer service desk, and they give you your money. Of course, they keep 10% for themselves. I know this doesn't make sense.... but, well, I just like to operate the machine.

I was at the counting machine Monday afternoon. There was a lady and her seven or eight-year-old son waiting behind me to use the machine. Beside of the change counting machine is a vending machine full of stuffed animals. You put fifty cents into the machine and use a remote-control hook type thing to retrieve a stuffed animal in a certain period of time. The little boy was standing by the stuffed animal machine with a look of awe and longing on face. You could tell that he wanted to give the machine a try.

The little boy looked a lot like I looked at that age. I knew exactly how much he wanted to try that machine. I've been there, folks. I told him to take fifty cents out of my Maxwell House container and give it a try. When I was almost through putting my money in the counting machine, his time ran out on the stuffed animal machine and I gave him fifty cents again. With that, I took my receipt into the store to collect my money.

As I was leaving the store, the little boy was helping his mother put her money into the counting machine. I could see that he did not win a stuffed animal and lamented, "Sorry you didn't win a stuffed animal." He replied, "I didn't really want a stuffed animal anyway… I just enjoyed trying to win one."

Yes, Sir, there is a lot of wisdom in that lad's words… he is wise beyond his years. What I took from his answer was, "In life, things don't always go your way… but enjoy the ride." Yep, wise beyond his years.

Don't watch the world go by… let the world watch you go by. bob

NAVY DAYS

PRETTY GIRL

This happened in Nha Be, Vietnam during Christmas of 1967 or 1968. I had worked all night and got back to the base at around 8AM. I tried to go to sleep, but was too tired. I took a shower, put on some clean clothes and went to the chow hall for something to eat. No one was there except the cooks, the Vietnamese helpers and a little blind girl who was the daughter of one of the helpers.

As I was leaving the chow-hall I got a small bag of oranges to take back to the barracks. I decided to stop and give one to this young girl. I must say she stole my heart. bob

ONE FOOT IN THE GRAVE

Things happen to me that would never happen to anyone else. It's my nature to laugh about it and go on.

I was just out of Navy boot camp and was reporting to my first duty station in Pensacola, Florida. Upon checking in, they told me that a retired Navy Chief Petty Officer had died and requested two people from our base to be Honor Guards. I was one of the lucky ones. He was to be buried two days later and the viewing was the next night at the funeral the following day.

We got on the bus and were on our way to Mobile, Alabama. We checked into a motel with the money they gave us, and later that evening we went to the funeral home for the viewing and introduced ourselves to the family. We were available to them for any of their needs. It ended up that all we had to do was fold the flag at the grave site and present it to the widow, "on behalf of a grateful nation."

The next morning, we took a taxi to the cemetery and waited for the proceedings to begin. After folding the flag, I was walked up to the widow to present her the flag, "on behalf of a grateful nation."

Well, the strangest thing happened. As I was delivering the flag to her, my left leg went down past the knee into the grave. Luckily, I was in the best shape of my life and was able not to fall down, and lifted myself up with my right leg. It seems that the grave was a little too large and the funeral home tried to cover in with green carpeting or AstroTurf. Without missing a beat, I delivered the flag to the widow. She thanked me and with a sweet smile on her face said, "Thank God your other leg wasn't on a banana peel."

There is humor in everything and I'm thankful that most of the people I know enjoy laughing and having fun. Those that don't enjoy it give me something else to laugh about. bob

LESSON LEARNED

Sometimes you learn lessons in the strangest of places. This story took place many years ago in Pensacola, Florida. I was a U.S. Navy Seaman Apprentice just out of basic training. I had volunteered for Vietnam duty and was temporarily assigned to Pensacola as they sorted out what they were going to do with me.

There was an oyster bar in Pensacola on the far end of the main street that ran right through town. It was a hangout for underage sailors and Marines because they would sell alcohol to anyone in uniform, regardless of your age. The legal drinking age was 21 and I was 19.

One Friday night I was sitting in there, eating oysters with a young man who was stationed aboard the USS Lexington. The "Lex" was a highly decorated aircraft carrier during World War ll. It was now very old and was used as a training carrier for Navy and Marine pilots.

As we were sitting there talking, I asked him, "What do you do aboard the "Lex'?" He explained that he had been on board for 6 months as a deck hand. He told me about scrubbing the deck every morning and evening and how he shined all the brass and metal to keep it from corroding, and that he also spent a lot of time painting. He then told me that "beginning Monday" he was going to work in the "radio shack" and begin on the job training to be a radioman.

To me being a radioman sounded better than being a deck hand, but he disagreed. He said that he wanted to be a deck hand for his entire enlistment, but they wouldn't let him. Of course, this made no sense to me.

He explained that as a deck hand he could stand back and look with pride at what he had done that day and actually see a job done well. He said that as a radioman he would not be able to do that. You know… after thinking about it, it made perfectly good sense to me.

After pondering about that for nearly 50 years, I am convinced that being a mom and a deck hand are the most important jobs you can have. After all, it is the deck hand that holds the ship together, and the mom holds the house together by cleaning, polishing, cooking, disciplining, and worrying, plus she does most of the child rearing. In other words, the mom cleans up most of the mess. The future of the world is in the hands of moms as far as I am concerned. Yes, a good mom can sure see the fruits of her labors… just like a deck hand, I suppose…bob

NAVY COFFEE

For some reason, many of you are talking about making and drinking coffee this morning. I guess that the cold weather and snow that we are having makes coffee taste even better.

During my Navy years I went through a lot of tough combat training, was shot at a few times, and was abused in many ways during that training. My worst treatment ever was over a pot of coffee.

I was in boot camp in Great Lakes, Illinois when the episode that I am about to tell you about happened.

I was standing the 0400 to 0600 watch, in the Master at Arms Office. My main duty was to answer the phone if it rang. Of course, the phone did not ring much at that hour and the Master at Arms, a second-class boatswain mate, and I just sat there and talked.

At about 0530, he asked me to make a pot of coffee. It was one of those silver coffee makers that was about 2 or 3 feet tall. I know you have all see those.

I took the coffee maker to the deep sink in the bathroom, dumped out the old coffee and grounds and proceeded to wash the coffee pot. The inside of the pot was black as if it had never been washed. I scrubbed and scrubbed with Ajax, trying to clean the pot… I was not making much headway… man, that thing was filthy.

After about 10 minutes, the Master at Arms came to check on me, because I was overdue getting back with the coffee. I have never seen anyone so irate in my life.

He grabbed me by the shoulders and was shaking me violently, with my head going back and forth like a bobble head. He yelled, "What is the matter with you… Do you want to get ' f in' kilt? …You never wash a coffee pot… it has been cured and you are washing the cure off of it."

When he finally turned me loose, the veins were still sticking out on his neck. He told me that the proper way to make coffee was just to add water to the pre-existing coffee and to add coffee grounds to the pre-existing grounds. He explained that, in the Navy, you never dump the old grounds out until there is no more room to add fresh coffee grounds.

I learned a lot in the Navy, but he was just wrong… wrong, but I did enjoy Navy coffee. A coffee pot does NOT need to be cured and it needs to be washed thoroughly with soap after each use… not just rinsed out. Now that is the truth. bob

LIBERTY IN SAIGON

It was probably about mid-October 1965. We were about ready to graduate from boot camp at the US Navy Training Center in Great Lakes, Illinois. We were finally close to the end of our training and got all day off on Sunday. We were required to go to church services, and during the afternoon we could do whatever we wanted as long as we stayed in or around our barracks.

David Sims, my first cousin, and I were sitting in a recreation room in the barracks. There was a record player with a few old scratchy records, a deck of cards, and some puzzles and board games. David and I were playing checkers and listening to the radio.

The radio announcer said that the US was building up troops in Vietnam and that more advisors were being sent to Saigon. David, in his usual positive way of looking at things said, "I bet Saigon is good liberty." I replied, "I would like to go there sometime." I do not know why I remember that brief conversation so vividly.

I really did want to go to Vietnam and about a year later, I put in a "chit" requesting to be sent to Vietnam with the Navy Amphibious Assault Group. It was approved and after much training, I was transferred to Nha Be, Vietnam, a River Patrol Base. Nha Be was located in the Mekong Delta, not far from Saigon. That was July of 1967.

In January of 1968 one of my friends and I asked for permission to go to Saigon for liberty. Saigon was an in-country R&R site. It was generally considered safe. Most of the troops who were stationed in Saigon lived in hotels and did not carry weapons.

A little after midnight, we were sitting on the roof of our hotel drinking beer and enjoying the safety of Saigon, when suddenly we heard small arms fire. We later learned that the airport was under attack... we really did not realize how bad things were and we soon went to bed.

When we awoke the next morning, we found out that the city was under siege. The TET Offensive had begun. The bus that was supposed to take us back to Nha Be was not running as scheduled. We called Nha Be and told them we could not get back on time. They told us to report for duty at the Naval Support Activity in Saigon and to get back to Nha Be whenever we could.

We got a ride to the Naval Support Activity with some MP's in an Army Jeep. When we reported to the Naval Support Activity, they assigned us to ride shotgun in vans that were hauling officers and other high-ranking civilians all over Saigon. Now that was an experience I will never forget. We did that for 2 or 3 days. I was scared to death the whole time. Things finally calmed down. There were just a few small skirmishes going on. Most of the VC had been either killed or run out of Saigon.

On our last day in Saigon, I was standing on the roof of the hotel looking out over the city. My friend was lying on a lawn lounge chair. Suddenly, a lone shot was fired, and at that same instant, a bullet whizzed just inches from the left side of my head. There was a lone sniper somewhere among those buildings that wanted one more kill, I guess. I am glad that it wasn't me. I sure was glad when we got back to Nha Be.

This story happened exactly 50 years ago today… and, David, if you are reading this from heaven, "liberty in Saigon ain't all that good." bob

VIETNAM VETS

Someone put a picture on Facebook this morning that said, "like and share if you respect our Vietnam Veterans." The picture depicted two elderly, overweight gentlemen wearing their Vietnam Veterans caps. Yeah, I 'spect that is how most of us look these days.

I choose to think of us the way we were during the war. We were all in great physical shape and willing to do whatever we had to do. We were all afraid from time to time, but we loved our country and were willing to try to help a foreign country remain free.

We wanted them to live a life like we have in the good old USA. We worked hard while over there, but we played hard as well.

We loved to get a little time off and go into Saigon and partake in all of the debauchery that the big city had to offer. We looked forward to R & R in places like Honolulu, Hong Kong, Tokyo, and Malaysia. I went to Bangkok. We also had in-country R & R in a place called Vung Tau. Vung Tau was a beautiful place, a tropical paradise... so near the war, but yet so far away.

When we left those R & R spots, our scared selves would return to the war zone and get the job done. Yeah, we lost that war, but it wasn't our fault. Then and now I take responsibility for my own actions... it was the fault of the game-playing politicians. Given the chance, the American fighting men would have won that war.

Being brave is not being fearless... being brave is being scared but doing it anyway. bob

THE DISMAL SWAMP

Another drizzly, rainy morning in the Carolinas today... thunderstorms expected later in the day.

Gaye went with me to check on the cows at our remote farm, and then we went to Tractor Supply. Gaye wanted some tomato stakes and I wanted some fly spray for the cows.

As we were riding the ATV across the dam beside the pond, we saw a big snapping turtle burrowed in... probably laying eggs. I guess with this being Memorial Day, and my mind sort of focused on the war, that turtle brought back some memories.

Before I went to Vietnam the first time, we had to take a course called SEE... Survival, Escape and Evasion. The final test was something that I enjoyed, but many did not make it through.

We took this training in Little Creek, Virginia. For the final test they dropped us into the Dismal Swamp. They gave us a map of where we were and it was our job to get back to a certain place while evading the "enemy" who was waiting along the route. The only food we had to eat was a candy bar. It was supposed to take a week to get back so we had to find our own food along the way as we tried to escape and evade.

Our candy bars did not last long, of course. For a week, our food consisted mainly of turtle, Polk salad, and occasionally wild berries. We would make stew out of the turtles. We would clean the turtle, drop it in boiling swamp water and eat it. I guess you would call it turtle stew. Sometimes the turtles would have eggs that we would drop into the soup... they gave it a little creaminess and substance, but not much. Polk Salad was much like turnip or mustard greens.

Most of you are near throwing up now, but if you are hungry, it tasted good. The thing I remember that I did not enjoy was the ticks. Each night we would check each other for ticks, and of course we all had them. One night a fellow pulled over 70 ticks off me.

Enough about that. bob

PARACHUTE RIGGERS

Captain Charlie Plumb was a Naval Aviator serving aboard the USS Kitty Hawk during the Vietnam War. He flew seventy-four successful combat missions and was shot down in enemy territory on his 75th mission, just a few days prior to finishing his tour of duty. He spent about seven years in various POW camps in North Vietnam.

Many years later, he was sitting in a restaurant when a man walked up to him and said, "You're Captain Plumb, aren't you?" Captain Plumb responded, "Yes, I am, how did you know?" The man answered, "I packed your parachute." Captain Plumb jumped up out of his seat and shook the man's hand vigorously as he thanked him. Captain Plumb did not even know the man when they were serving together, but that man made a big difference in Captain Plumb's life.

I can't help but wonder about things sometimes... I wonder how many "parachute riggers" in my life go un-thanked... I need to work on that. Equally important... Have I packed anyone's parachute today?

Just a little food for thought. bob

CHRISTMAS PAST

THE CHRISTMAS OF 1966

The Vietnam War was beginning to escalate, and I had volunteered. I had already passed the mental test to prove that I was crazy and was awaiting orders for the rest of the training in Little Creek, Va. If all went as I planned, I would be in Vietnam by summer.

I told my parents that I would hitchhike home for Christmas leave. I planned leave at daybreak on the Saturday before Christmas. I was unable to sleep so I left shortly after midnight. The first car that I thumbed picked me up and had a baby in the back seat in a plastic tub of some kind. The baby started crying and the mother handed me a bottle and told me to feed the baby. When I finished, they gave me a McDonald's hamburger… my first ever. They took me to Greenville, SC and the next car took me all the way to my parents door.

No one was home so I went on in and went to bed. I woke up at around 6PM to the sound of many people in the house. I heard someone say, "Alice, he'll be OK." I got up and went into the kitchen and there was probably 20 or so people that had come to welcome me home. Mom had NO IDEA I was in my room and she was worried.

I really felt the love that Christmas from everyone...like never before. Seven months later I had completed all my training and was in Vietnam. During the 18 months that I was there, I often thought of the warmth that everyone showed me. I never forgot the wonderful smell of baby oil and powder from that baby and how secure it made me feel. I can never thank my family and friends enough for all the love. I pray that each of you somehow can feel that same love that I felt that Christmas and continue to feel today. Merry Christmas. bob

CHRISTMAS CIRCA 1990

One morning in September, a young lady named Beverly came into my office. I had met her and knew her. We were acquaintances, not really friends. It seems that Beverly had acquired some land on the top of Barrett's Mountain and two cows came with the land. She wanted to know if I would take a bull up there and breed them for her. I told her, "No, that I didn't like the idea of taking a bull up there with no one to look after it." I did, however, agree to go up there and get her cows, bring them to my home farm, and return them after they were bred.

I kept her cows for about 70 days which would give them 3 cycles in which to get pregnant.

It was on a cold Saturday morning when I decided to return them to Barrett's Mountain, less than 2 weeks before Christmas. An old friend of mine, Ronnie Deese, wanted to go along for the ride. We had been friends all through high school and remain so today. We attend the same church, and he lives close to us. As always, we were in search of adventure, a new friend, or maybe a memory. As luck would have it, we found all three.

Barrett's Mountain is in a neighboring county and it about 1/2 mile high. At the time it had a narrow, winding dirt road with a few gravel thrown in to take you to the summit. We were about halfway up the mountain when the truck lost traction. The strangest thing happened. The cows had moved to the back of the trailer and it caused the back wheels of the truck to lose contact with the road because of the uneven weight distribution. We tried to get the cows to the front of the trailer, but they wouldn't stay. Our only option was to walk to the bottom of the mountain and find someone to pull us to the top with a tractor.

We hit pay dirt at the first house. The man came to the door, but said he could not help us because he had a lung removed that week, but we were welcome to use his tractor if it would start. He said the tractor hadn't been cranked since August and sure enough, it would not start. He said, "Well, it looks like you are going to have to use my 4-wheel drive truck." That man did not know us from Adam and trusted us with his truck. No questions asked. The truck started and we were easily able to get the cows back to their proper pasture.

I never wanted to get stuck like that again so I bought a new 4-wheel drive truck that week. It was my first 4-wheel drive and I never have understood how I got along without one all those years.

As Ronnie and I were on the way home, we decided to take the man a Christmas gift the next Saturday. We returned with a flannel shirt, a pair of gloves, and one of those cheese and salami gift boxes. He expressed his gratitude to us and was very thankful. He couldn't believe that two strangers would bring him a Christmas gift.

It was a cold, rainy night about two months later when there was a knock on our door. It was two young ladies whose truck was stuck in our garden. They explained that they had just mo-ved into our community and were riding around to see the area. They thought my drive way was a state road, and when they rea-lized that it wasn't, they tried to turn around. Not being able to see well because of the weather, they backed off an embankment and got stuck up.

They wanted to know if I would pull them out with my tractor. I told them, "No, I have an upper respiratory infection, but you are more than welcome to use my tractor." They had no idea how to drive a tractor and I started to have thoughts of two months prior......"Well, I said, looks like you are going to have to use my truck." They said they had no idea how to attach a chain without damaging something. I said, "Just take my truck home with you and come back tomorrow when you get off work and I will pull your truck out in the morning when I feel better." They came back the next day and gave me a pair of leather dress gloves with rabbit fur lining. Those were the best gloves I have ever owned.

I trust people....to a fault. I have lost a lot because of it, but I have gained much more. We all feel a sense of unity during the Christmas season, but we sometimes lose it for the rest of the year. Let's take a lesson from the giant sequoia trees in Califor-nia. Those trees are often 300 feet tall and 30 feet in diameter. They live to be 300 years old. The interesting thing is that their roots only go down for 3 feet. You never see a sequoia tree fall down from high winds like you do most other trees." "Why," you ask? All of the sequoia roots spread outward and intermesh with the roots of the other trees and they support one another. It reminds me of the old saying, "one for all and all for one." This year, let's be the best friend we can be. Love one another. Open your arms and embrace one another, just like the roots of a sequoia tree.

Love one another just as Jesus taught us. Like all of you, I love to receive and give Christmas gifts, but remember the true reason for Christmas. It is Jesus' birthday. Worship and celebrate His life. After all, He gave you the greatest gift of all… eternal life. All you have to do is accept Him as your Savior. I hope you will bow your head right now and ask Him into your life. bob

CHRISTMAS 1963

My neighbor had quite a collection of rifles. He had recently bought a new one that he was quite proud of. It was only a 22, but he was proud of the way it loaded. It loaded through the wooden stock and would hold 15 long rifle rounds. I wanted one just like it for Christmas.

When I came home from my after school, part-time job at the Winn-Dixie one day, my dad and our neighbor, F. E. Thornburg, were standing in F.E.'s yard talking. When they saw me, F.E. ran into the house trying to conceal a long, brown object. I knew that it was the rifle. I figured Dad had gone over there to look at it and when they saw me, they tried to hide what they were doing. I knew then that I was going to get a rifle like that for Christmas.

I could not wait for Christmas morning because I knew that long, narrow box under the tree contained my rifle. I got up early on Christmas morning, opened my rifle, loaded it, and jumped into my Volkswagen. I was on my way to my cousin, Connie Beckham's house to fire that rifle. You see, our family lived in the city limits where it was illegal to fire a gun. Connie lived on Route 2 where shooting a gun was permissible. I was on my way to yet another adventure.

There were no one-way streets in Newton at the time. I was going north from my home on South Main Avenue. When I got to

"A" street, I turned right onto the courthouse square beside of Sanitary Grocery. As I made the righthand turn, I lost control of the VW and spun out on some ice that was still there from a freezing rain storm we had a few days prior... There was no damage done and there was not a car in sight... except one... a policeman named Don, the only policeman on duty that Christmas morning in our small town. He saw the whole thing.

Of course, I was not in any trouble. Don wanted to know what I was doing out so early. I told him about the rifle. He had never seen one like that and wanted to try it out. I told him it was loaded and ready to go. He cocked it and fired about 10 rounds into a tree on the court house lawn. He handed it back to me and I shot at the street light right in front of Sanitary Grocery. I figured that if he could shoot in the city limits, I could too. He said we needed to move on before we cause some real damage.

I finally got to Connie's house and her husband, Doug, and I went out to fire the rifle. We shot at trees and fence posts for a while and were getting the feel of the rifle.

There was a sheet blowing in the wind on the clothes line. Doug said that he had always heard that if you shot a sheet blowing on a clothes line that a 22 cartridge would not penetrate it. One of us shot the sheet, but we do not remember if it made a hole.

I asked Connie about it recently. She said she remembered me being over there with a rifle, but did not remember anything about the sheet. I asked Doug at the Old Soldiers Reunion, and he said that he remembered the incident, but did not think it made a hole because Connie would have never let us forget it. I am thinking that it did make a very small hole. I seem to remember Doug saying, "Connie will never know the difference unless she sticks her toe in the hole and tears the sheet." It really doesn't matter at this point about the sheet… we have a lot more important things to think about.

This story is about southern small town living in the 60's… not sheets. It was a great time to be alive, and with all the troubles and problems I see around the nation and the world today, I would give up my "so called" modern conveniences to go back to those days.

Hopefully, you enjoyed this story. As we look back and reminisce this time of year, let's reflect on the good. As we go through our daily lives, let's remember that Jesus was born on Christmas day and was brought into this world to die and save us from our sins. That is what Christmas is about. You know, as Christians we are all winners… there are no losers, so do not despair. Remember that, and please accept Him as your personal Savior if you haven't already done so. bob

CHRISTMAS GIFTS

We make a big deal out of Christmas gift giving in our family. That is not my preference, but that is the way it works out.

Usually at this time of the year, I ask Justin to email me a list of what he wants, with links to a website, and I order it. Gaye always gives me a list and I get what she wants…plus a few surprises.

Well, I am different. I have everything that I need and want, and never tell them what I want because……shoot, I do not even know. My wants and needs are small. I just leave it up to them. It does not matter to me.

My glasses are worn out, to say the least, and Gaye was riding with me to Treasure's to get new ones. On the way to Treasure's, she said she would like for me to take her to some stores that I like and give her an idea of Christmas gifts for me. I did not like that idea.

I told her she could just pay for my glasses and that would be my gift. She said, "That would not be much of a gift." Maybe not, but it would have suited me just fine. In my odd, out-of-the-box way of thinking, it took me back to the old days of the 50's, and I was reminded of my dad.

In the early days, when Dad was struggling, he thought that gifts for my mother needed to be practical. He would buy her things like brooms and dish towels for Christmas. Well, that is not much of a gift either.

As our economic situation improved, he changed a lot. One time about this time of the year in 1962, Mama had gone to Atlanta to visit my sister. He and I were trying to hold down the fort without the help of Mom. About 7AM one morning, the phone rang. I answered and it was Mom. We talked a few minutes, and then she wanted to talk to Daddy. I put him on and in a few minutes, he came back into the kitchen laughing. I said, "What is so funny?" He said that Mom had seen a mink stole in a store down there for $1800 that she wanted for Christmas. "What are you going to do?" I asked. He said, "I am going to Western Union and wire her the money… she said she was not going to come home unless I sent it."

A couple years later, he got her the finest Gibson guitar that I had ever seen. That thing sounded better than any of my Martins. When she played that thing, it sounded like an Angel Hand Bell orchestra. That was the first good guitar that mom had ever owned, and she sat around playing that thing all the time. What a great gift.

We put waaaay too much emphasis on gifts. Wish we didn't. The best gift we can receive is the gift of Jesus. That is what it is all about anyway. Do not forget that. bob

A CHRISTMAS STORY 2015

When I woke up this morning, I thought the day would just be a routine Saturday, but it ended up being extra special to me. Let me tell you a little about it.

When I was a youngster, Mama made even the smallest event seem exciting. Christmas, Halloween, Thanksgiving, and birthdays were all very special. Mama had a way of building up anticipation in us kids. With Mama, even a trip to the dentist was fun.

Gaye and I decided to go to the Christmas parade in Taylorsville, NC today. We always look forward to the parade every year. At this parade, the adults usually sit behind the sidewalk in someone's yard, and the children are on the sidewalk or curb to have better access to the candy that the parade participants throw to them.

While we were waiting for the parade, Gaye observed that a certain little boy on the sidewalk looked a lot like me when I was that age. She was right. He not only looked like me, but he acted like me. With eager anticipation, he kept running to the edge of the street awaiting the first glimpse of the parade. He finally saw it coming and with wide eyes exclaimed, "Here it comes now!!!!" Yep, that little boy was me.

It only took a few minutes until his Dollar General bag was almost half filled with candy. Then something unusual happened.

Out of all the people sitting around there, he came up to me and said, "Sir, would you like a piece of candy?" I told him that,

"I would appreciate a Tootsie Roll." Looking through his bag he finally found one and handed it to me. From that point on, every time he got a Tootsie Roll, he would throw it to me. He just seemed happy to share with me. Again, I do not know why he picked me.

When the parade ended, I wanted to reward the lad. As I walked by him on the way to the car, I handed him a five-dollar bill. The look on his eyes was priceless to me. Those big eyes and that mouth hanging agape spoke to me, reminding me of a time long, long, ago. He thanked me, hugged me, and ran to his parents and friends excitedly saying, "Look what I have"… just like I would have done.

Yes, he sure did bring back memories to me from long ago. I could just see Mama sitting there chuckling at my excitement and antics.

Peace on earth and good will toward men would be a great Christmas gift. Somehow, that is what that lad gave me a little of in his own special way. bob

PATIENCE AT CHRISTMAS

Patience!!!! That is something that most children do not have much of during the Christmas season. Christmas could never get here soon enough for me. I would get all antsy and just couldn't wait for Santa.

When Mom and Dad weren't around, my sister and I would prowl around in their bedroom looking for Christmas gifts. One year we found a box of chocolate covered cherries. We decided to eat the bottom layer, put the top layer back on, and during the excitement of Christmas morning, no one would know the difference. You see, we had no patience… we just couldn't wait.

Now-a-days I am very patient. When we first moved here in 1976, the house was about 60 years old. Believe me, remodeling old houses takes plenty of patience. Putting in a new heating system was one of the first things on our agenda as we began remodeling.

We hired a local heating contractor to do the work. When we got home one day, he had removed the old furnace, but had not installed the new one. I figured that he would finish the next day. When he didn't come the next day, I gave him a call to see what was going on. He said that the furnace he had planned to install wouldn't work, and he was going to have to order a different kind.

To make a long story short, it took SEVEN years for them to find a new system. During those seven years, we heated entirely with a wood stove. Carl Rector said, "Every time I see you coming out of the woods with a chain saw and axe, I think of Alley Oop." That proves I am patient.

For the last several weeks, Gaye has been asking me what I want Christmas. My needs and wants are few. I wanted a few packs of Martin guitar strings, some stiff flat picks, and a sampler box of canned goods from <u>Stan Hitchcock</u>. The sampler box contains Caramel Pecan Apple Butter, Sweet Heat Salsa, and old-fashioned Pure Sorghum. Gaye told me to order it from Stan's Facebook page since she doesn't do Facebook. The package arrived a few days later.

I wanted to try the sorghum right then. I went to the kitchen to bake a pan of biscuits. I just couldn't wait to sop that sorghum with fresh, hot biscuits. I looked into the living room as I was baking the biscuits and there sat Gaye on the floor wrapping the sampler box. I tried to stop her. "No, don't do that," I pleaded,

"I'm baking biscuits to try the sorghum for lunch." She said, "That is your Christmas present, you are going to have to wait until Christmas." "But I am a big boy now, I don't have to wait," I responded. She informed me that the reason I have to wait, "is because you ARE a big boy now." I guess she told me. Seventeen more days and counting. I can't wait... maybe I'm not as patient as I thought I was. bob

CHRISTMAS ON THE MILL HILL

This story goes back to the 50's when life was good and the living was easy. My family had moved into the first house that we actually owned, and not an old mill house provided by the mill where Daddy worked. Most of the families in town were just like us. The war had not been over very long, and everyone was trying to find their place in the world.

Christmas was a big deal for us kids around town. Most of us did not get many toys and treats except for Christmas and our birthdays.

On Christmas Eve everyone in our family would gather at my grandfather's house, and all of my cousins and I would share a little gift of some kind. All of the Sims family were musically inclined... and pretty soon someone would break out a guitar or mandolin and the music would begin. What a time we had.

We would usually get home at about 9PM and my sister and I would go straight to bed so mom and dad could prepare things for Christmas morning. We knew that Santa would not come if we were awake.

I was always too excited to sleep, and I would usually get up at about 2AM and open my presents.

On this particular Christmas morning, I ran into the living room and right there on the table was a bowl of M & M's, a bowl of English walnuts, and that familiar red and white box of chocolate covered cherries. I ate some of each of them and fell to my knees and crawled around the tree to see what my gifts were.

There were two packages with my name on them. As I tore them open, I was overwhelmed that I got a pair of cowboy chaps and a Howdy Doody hand puppet. I could not wait to go outside to play. I put on my flannel cowboy shirt, my cowboy boots, hat. and my new chaps. I then strapped on my six shooter, put my Howdy Doody puppet on my left hand and ran outside to play… I did not wear my Red Ryder gloves with the fringe on the side because that would hamper my using my new Howdy Doody hand puppet. In my mind I was Wild Bill Hickok.

When I got outside it was dark and cold… Cold. The first thing I heard was the Burgess boys who lived across the road. They were running up and down the street hollering and yapping to the top of their voices. When they came into view, they were wearing loin cloths that they got for Christmas. I guess they were home-made because I do no remember seeing them in stores. That is all that they had on. Since I had my cowboy clothes on and they were dressed like the TV Indians… we were ready to play. We were all excited that we were all dressed to play our cowboy and Indian roles…

After a few minutes, the Burgess boys wanted to show me their other Christmas gifts. They each got a trapeze bar and a piece of rope that they could tie onto a tree limb and swing like Burt Lancaster and Tony Curtis who starred in the movie "Trapeze" which was popular at the time.

One of the Burgess boys hung by his legs on the trapeze bar, and the loin cloth flopped down over his stomach (you will have to visualize here) and he was buck naked under that loin cloth. That is all I will say about that. I knew how cold I was, and I felt that he must have been freezing.

I went back into the house to enjoy some more candy and nuts. When I looked down, my chaps were missing. Somehow, I did not tighten that slide fastener properly that held them around my waist. It had come loose and my chaps fell to the ground during our ordeal. I was so excited that I did not realize it had happened. The main reason that I was so cold is because I did not know that you were supposed to wear jeans under your chaps. I was buck naked from the waist down except for my boots. I found my chaps in the yard and hurried back into the house. By about 6AM the young'uns were running everywhere up and down the street showing off their new toys.

We were not a poor family by any means. This was simply the way people lived in those days. We had everything we needed and more. It was a time that neighbors and friends were true friends and neighbors, not just someone who lived beside you or someone you were acquainted with. We often hear the expression, "I got your back." In those days, it was more-true than ever. bob

TWO GOOD CHRISTMAS GIFTS

While I was at the other farm feeding and checking on the cows, our neighbors Randy and Robin brought us some homemade candy. It is a variety of nuts covered in dark chocolate. Oh Lord, they are good. Thanks for that. Nothing like good neighbors.

I returned home and… lo and behold, our friend Michael Smith dropped by. He had been fishing and brought us a mess of crappie for Christmas. I have already cleaned them and Gaye is putting them in the freezer bags. They will make several good meals later on this winter.

Just country people doing what they do best... loving one another. bob

THE SCHMIDT HOUSE

It has always amazed me how Santa locates the homes of the good little boys and girls on Christmas Eve as he makes his rounds delivering Christmas gifts to them. He has done that for several hundred years without incident... well, there was that one year...

On Christmas Eve afternoon in 1868, Santa and Mrs. Claus were very busy getting everything ready for Santa's world-wide trip. They had washed and waxed the sleigh, greased the runners, fed and harnessed the reindeer, and loaded the sleigh with gifts. Santa gave Mrs. Claus a farewell kiss and he was on his way.

Santa had finished his deliveries in Europe and was crossing the Atlantic Ocean, approaching the North Carolina shoreline... when suddenly it happened...

The sleigh went down and crashed into an outhouse. Sleigh parts, toys, and injured reindeer were flying all over the place. When Santa finally regained consciousness, he angrily approached Rudolph and said, "Rudolph, I told you to go the SCHMIDT house." bob

CHEX MIX

Dadgum, I am in trouble again!!

Gaye makes a Chex Mix thing for one of her sisters every Christmas. Gaye uses 3 kinds of Chex cereal and every kind of nut you can think of. She douses them with some liquid concoction that she dreamed up and then bakes it. Her sister thinks it is something special... and I guess it is, compared to others that I have eaten.

Somehow or the other all of the pecans, cashews, and almonds disappeared out of it today while Gaye was away from sunrise until after dark. I had an alibi... I was in the bedroom painting just about all day.

I think I saw a mouse in the kitchen. It was moving so quickly that I didn't know for sure what it was... I am not sure if I even saw it. Man, that thing was fast... or someone could have come into the house while I was painting. I was so absorbed in my painting that I probably wouldn't have heard them.

For whatever reason, she thinks I am the guilty party... Everybody knows I wouldn't do a thing like that. Our dog houses are full. Anyone got a trailer for sale or rent... or a room to let for fifty cents? bob

CHRISTMAS WITH CHILDREN

Gaye and I got to do one of our favorite Christmas things today. One of Justin's best friends from high school lives near us. We traditionally take their three children, ages 8, 11, and 13, out for lunch and then shopping.

Today we first went to Wendy's. I was impressed that one of them got apple slices. I do not remember what the others got... probably not quite so healthy.

The next stop was Walmart. We gave each of the children $25. We put the money in their hands and made them responsible for it. The deal is that they can buy anything they want but cannot exceed the $25. If they spend less than $25, they can keep the change.

Talk about good shoppers. You should have seen them going through the aisles of Walmart looking at the prices of things before they made their selections. They just about wore me out. They took me to places in Walmart that I didn't even know were there. They soon made their choices… and we were off on our way…

The next stop was Margaret's Country Store for ice cream. We all had a cone. I had "birthday cake ice cream." I had never had that before… pretty good.

When we dropped them off at home, it thrilled me to see those happy youngsters bouncing into the house with their gifts. Reminded me of me when I was that age.

What a great and joyous day for Gaye and me. We enjoyed it more than they did. I hope they will remember this as a great Christmas memory. bob

IF EVERY DAY COULD BE LIKE CHRISTMAS+---

Well, Christmas has come and gone, but as much as I love Christmas, I had to breathe a sigh of relief when it was over. We just absolutely overdo it at our house.

I got to thinking about what I like most about Christmas, aside for the fact that Jesus was born.

I think what I like most is the positive change that I see in some people.

On Saturday morning I came into contact with a fellow that I know. We are not exactly friends… we have very little in common. We simply just know each other. This man is an atheist and proudly proclaims it around me. I have often thought that he is trying to provoke an argument, but I avoid that. Anyway, when I saw him Saturday, he gave me a big hug and wished me a Merry Christmas with a very warm smile on his face. I liked that.

I then went to Walmart to buy some potato sticks and cashews to add to the Chex Mix that a mouse, rat, squirrel, or <u>Larry Eckard</u> ate while Gaye was out of town. I easily found the cashews, but I was having trouble finding the potato sticks.

I was standing in the potato chip section, looking for the potato sticks. Apparently, time got away from me and I had been standing there for a few minutes looking confused. A lady, not an employee, walked up to me and asked if she could help me. After telling her what I was looking for, she took me by the hand and led me all the way to the other end of the aisle where the Pringles were located. I have no idea why potato sticks are not located with the potato chips. Anyway, she found an oatmeal-sized box of potato sticks for me. I thanked her. She gave me a beautiful smile and wished me a joyful Christmas. I sure did feel good about that. It made my day even better.

Anyway… it got me to thinking about how nice everyone is this time of year. All that I could think of was that the name and thought of Jesus changes people. Some for just a few weeks a year....and some for a lifetime. bob

THE ENCOUNTER

When he awoke that morning, he just did not feel well. There was a gnawing in his stomach that was not from a physical ailment, but one of homesickness… out of control homesickness. It was his first Christmas away from home.

When he got out of his bunk, he looked around and felt even lonelier. His roommates and friends had gone home for Christmas.

He had only been in the Navy for four months and had not accumulated enough leave to go home. There was only a skeleton crew on base. He felt alone and lonely. You can be alone and not be lonely, but it is horrible to be both alone and lonely. At the time, he didn't know that you are never alone.

He put on his clothes and walked to the chow hall. He got a bowl of oatmeal and a glass of milk… thinking that would settle his stomach. It didn't… he took a bite or two and went back to his barracks.

He went to a pay phone and made a collect call to his parents. His mom told him about the good time they had on Christmas Eve with extended family… the music, the food, the gifts. His sister and her family were home from Pennsylvania. They had just finished Mom's big Christmas breakfast and were getting ready to open gifts. The whole family was together. Oh, how he longed to be with them. After they finished the phone call, he actually felt worse and the gnawing in his stomach intensified.

He sat around the barracks for the rest of the morning reading magazines and listening to the non-stop Christmas music that the local country music station was playing. At about noon, he decided to get a taxi and go to town. There was an oyster bar that he liked where you could always find a friend.

When the taxi got him to town… it was a ghost town. All of the stores were closed and there were few cars on the road and no pedestrian traffic. He decided to walk down to the end of the street near the municipal auditorium and sit on a bench overlooking Pensacola Bay and spend some time reflecting.

When he got near the auditorium, it was unusual to see a lone girl sitting on a bench. "May I join you?" he asked. "YOU'RE

IN THE NAVY," she quickly snapped. It was easy to tell that. Although he was wearing civilian clothing, his close-cropped hair and spit-shined shoes gave him away. He told her that he didn't bite and she reluctantly said, "Well, sit down then." She probably thought that sitting with one of those heathen sailors was a little better than sitting alone. He later found out that she was alone, and lonely as well.

She was from southern Florida and was a student at PJC, Pensacola Junior College. PJC students were, I believe, told to "stay away from those heathen sailors." There was always an air of contention between sailors and PJC students. After talking for an hour or so, they decided to walk back to town. She told him that her father was the pastor of a church, and the well-meaning congregation gave he and his wife a ticket for a 10-day tour in the Holy Land for Christmas. PJC had closed completely down for Christmas and she was staying with an old couple from the church she was attending.

As they were walking back to town, he felt her slip her arm around his waist. He, taking the hint, put his arm around her shoulder. It was nothing romantic, they both just needed someone to feel close to.

When they got back to town, the café beside the Saenger Theater had opened. They went in for a hamburger and coke and talked for about another hour. When they left the café, she said she had to get back to the couple she was staying with. They gave each other a farewell hug and a kiss on the cheek and started walking in different directions... neither looking back. Sometimes two opposites attract... if only for a few hours.

She probably had a car parked somewhere around there, and he started walking the 4-mile trek back to his base. He had spent his taxi fare on her hamburger and coke. That was all the money he had.

That day was a learning experience for both of them. She learned that all sailors aren't bad, and he learned that some nice people attended PJC. There is good in everyone, even PJC students and sailors.

He has never forgotten how it feels to be alone and lonely at Christmas. In fact, he continues to visit the hospital and lonely people on Christmas to this day. His life was greatly enriched by that chance encounter over 50 years ago. bob

THE ULTIMATUM

Well, I never would have thought it would come down to this… not in the Marlowe household.

I remember our first Christmas together… 48 years ago. We were living in a little housing development and had purchased our first Christmas tree. It was an artificial Christmas tree from Kmart. It was a cheap thing. Cheap and inexpensive are two different things. This thing was CHEAP. After all, we had those high $130 a month house payments for our new house. That tree was the best we could afford.

It was raining one Saturday afternoon, Gaye had gone Christmas shopping and I needed something to do. I wanted to surprise Gaye so I assembled and decorated that Christmas tree. It was a beautiful thing……at least to me.

Gaye soon arrived home and I took her by the hand, led her into the living room and excitedly showed her our tree. Her faced drooped and she looked as if she was going to cry. I thought that she was overwhelmed at the fine job I had done and the beauty of it all.

Later that evening, Gaye took all the decorations off the tree, rebent the limbs and redid the tree. She did not want my help. To be honest, it did look a lot better. It was at that moment that I realized that I needed to leave the tree decorating to Gaye. Admittedly, mine looked like a Charlie Brown Christmas tree.

In the following years, Gaye always did the decorating without any help from me. When Justin got old enough, he always enjoyed helping her. When Justin left the nest in 1995, she continued to do the decorating alone.

Many years ago, we started buying real Christmas trees. We enjoy the smell of the balsam fir wafting throughout the house.

Just yesterday, Gaye gave me THE ULTIMATUM. She said it was time to purchase our tree. She further stated, "If you do not help me decorate it, I am going to buy one of those fine pre-lit and fully-decorated artificial trees, I am too busy this year to spend all that time decorating a live tree." I told her that a tree like that would be fine with me.

Truthfully, that was not fine with me. I began to feel anxious and a gnawing began inside my stomach. Honestly, I did not want to give up our tradition of having a live tree. I did not know what to do.

After prayer, supplication, and 37 minutes of fasting, I told her that I would help her decorate a real live tree. I do not know how this is going to work out. I am hoping for a Holy Ghost intervention. bob

FRIENDS REMEMBERED

REMEMBERING GARY

I first met Gary in the fall of 1999, He was working as a short order cook in the old pool room in Newton. I was the only one in there early one Saturday morning. He said he was a painter by profession and was only working there to earn a little extra money. I asked him to come by and give me a quote on painting my house. He and a friend came by that afternoon and quoted $500 and for me to furnish the paint. That was an incredible price, actually too good to be true so I hired him.

He quit his job at the pool room and started painting on Monday morning. He painted for an hour or two and then began helping me do maintenance and repair around the farm. That's the way it was from that point on. He would paint a while and farm a while.

He was just like a member of the family and basically moved in with us. He lived with his teenage daughter who was supposed to bring him to work every day and then pick him up, but most of the time she did not show up so he just stayed with us. He did not have a car.

One day Gaye, or Miss Gaynell as Gary called her, baked a pineapple upside down cake. Gary had never had one before and ate the whole thing in one sitting.

Another time some of my friends from Waynesville and Rob-binsville were down here to deer hunt. Gary was frying cat fish for everyone. Everyone was bragging about how good they were. Gary said the key was to put a little Texas Pete in the batter. He was so proud of himself.

When Gary finished painting the house about 8 weeks later, I wrote his check but he wanted cash. He said the bank would charge him to cash it because he didn't have an account… I told him that I would take him to the bank and would get it cashed free. When they asked for his ID, he sheepishly said all he had was his prison ID. I didn't ask any questions.

For the next few years, Gary would drop by for a visit every few months if he could get someone to bring him. His visits gradually slowed down, eventually to none at all. We always enjoyed having him.

The last time I saw Gary was about 2 years ago. He surprised us by dropping by one Sunday afternoon to thank us and to tell us that he had gotten saved.

This past winter, I read Gary's obituary in the paper. It didn't say much… just that he had died and was going to be buried. Gary's life was not all that great in the eyes of the world but my life was greatly enriched by knowing Gary. bob

REMEMBERING BRADSHER

When you get to be my age, the only reason you subscribe to the newspaper is to read the obituaries and perhaps the sports. I have noticed many young people passing on in recent days. It reminded me of some of my friends who have left us way to soon.

My thoughts went all the way back to when I was in the seventh and eighth grades at South Newton Elementary. There were only about 25 people in our class and we were all close and intimate friends. We would go to each other's homes to play and there were no cliques. We were all friends... except for Bradsher.

Bradsher was a couple years older than the rest of us. He was bigger and stronger. Bradsher had homemade tattoos, ducktail haircut, pegged jeans, taps on his shoes, and was not very sociable. Those were sure signs of a juvenile delinquent. Bradsher's friends were a group of high school drop outs that he would spend time with in town. Bradsher rarely did his homework and would sit behind the map stand at the back of the room.

In the 7th grade we were studying about electricity and we had to do a project in electricity. I remember that I made a working telegraph with a few blocks of wood, some wire, a tin can, and a dry cell battery. Bradsher found this thing along the rail road tracks that had a wire attached to it. He decided to take it home and attach it to a dry cell battery and use that as his project.

He took it home, went to his room and there was a tremendous explosion. It was a dynamite cap. It blew one of his eyes out and inflicted many other injuries.

The local hospital was only a few blocks from our school and we would walk to the hospital every day after school to visit him When he got out of the hospital and got back to school, we saw a different Bradsher. He found out for the first time that we cared and were concerned about his welfare.

The last time that I had any interaction with him was on the first day of school in the 9th grade. It those days it was acceptable for seniors to haze freshmen. My sister was a senior and many of the senior boys would come to our house and I knew them all.

All summer long they jokingly told me that they would get me on the first day of school... but I knew they were serious.

We were standing in front of the school that morning when one senior came behind me with a bear hug and another one attacked me from the front. They said they were going to take my pants off and run them up the flag pole. I was fighting back. Bradsher walked over and told them to leave me alone and not to touch anyone else from South Newton. They tucked tail and disappeared never to touch any of us again.

Bradsher quit school toward the end of the 9th grade. He got married, got a job at Carolina Mills, and moved into a duplex in South Newton. I would see him occasionally as he rode by. I thought he was doing well.

One morning I awoke to the news that Bradsher had taken his own life. Those of us who really knew him were greatly saddened.

I learned some lessons from Bradsher. Never judge someone, you never know what they are going through. Never take your friends for granted. There is good in everyone. God loves all his children equally, we should as well.

Try to love the unlovely. It's been fifty years... and I will never forget Bradsher Lee Adcock. bob

REMEMBERING MR. MAUNEY

When I bought our first farm in 1975, I didn't have any idea what I was getting into. I knew nothing about farming, but I had always found farming to be interesting... So why not give it a try.

My closest neighbor was a big black man of over 300 pounds who worked on an adjoining farm. He was a gentle giant.

When we first moved into our new home, he was the first neighbor to visit us. He said to" let me know if we ever needed any help."

At the time, in addition to cattle I grew corn, soy beans, and small grain. On the day that I was preparing to plant my first crop, he just happened to show up to make sure I had all of my equipment set right to get me off on the right foot.

I never asked him for help, he just had some uncanny way of knowing when I could use his advice and help. That's the way it is supposed to be, friends helping friends. He would never take any pay, but he liked Schlitz beer and I would get him a quart or two fairly often.

One day we were working on a combine and this really fat guy rode up on a moped wanting to know if he could go fishing. Maybe an hour later that guy came riding by where we were working. He had caught a cooter (large turtle) and tied it to the back fender of his moped. The turtle was still alive and stretching its head out of the shell and trying to bite the fat boy on the butt. Most of the fat boys butt was sticking out of the top of his pants. We both had to lie down on the dirt floor and laugh. You need to visualize.

One year I decided to sow grass and to build fences around everything I owned and get out of the crop business and breed cows only. I wanted my last corn crop to be a good one and it was. My neighbor introduced me to a fellow from the mountains who wanted to buy my entire corn crop to make corn meal with his water powered grist mill to sell to the tourist. Later that fall my neighbor and I drove up there to see the grist mill and it wasn't a grist mill at all. It was a moonshine still. We did get a quart of moonshine.

This is eerie… I was helping him feed his cows one day and a bale of hay in the far corner of the barn fell for no apparent reason. He told me to finish loading the hay in the truck because he needed to go to the house. When he got to the house, the phone rang and someone told him that his mother had just died. That falling bale was a sign to him.

During his last years, he was confined to the house after suffering a stroke. We would buy groceries for them, and just last week, I took them some fresh veggies from the garden. They were very poor and always appreciative. I wish that I would have done more for that fine man, but it's too late now.

Today he went home to be with the Lord. Rest in peace, my fine friend, Lyndon (L) Mauney. bob

REMEMBERING DAVID

David Sims was my cousin and best friend. From the time we were little boys, we had plans to join the Navy on the "Buddy System". That simply meant that we would go through boot camp together. We took over Company 383 in Great Lakes, Illinois. David was the Recruit Chief Petty Officer and I was the Recruit Master at Arms. For some reason, we were feared by the other recruits. After we left boot camp we went in different directions.

When I was home on leave prior to my first visit to Vietnam, David was stationed in Williamsburg, Virginia so I went up to visit him for the weekend. I cannot tell you very much about the things we did because the Statute of Limitations might not be up yet. David lived off base in an apartment and we wanted to grill steaks for two girls that we had met. We did not have much money so we sneaked into the chow hall on his base and "borrowed" four pretty good steaks. After we grilled them, we realized we did not have any steak knives so we used one pair of scissors that we passed around the table to cut our steaks with. I wish I could tell you all of our adventures on that weekend.

David passed away a couple of years ago and I miss him as much as I do Mom and Dad.

David Sims, US Navy. August 6,1965 through. August 5, 1969. bob

REMEMBERING STEVE

Steve was not an ordinary person......he was extraordinary

He had been raised all his life to trust in God, be positive and to do the best you can with what you have to work with. There was no way he would let his disabilities stop him from being the best he could be. He never asked, "Why me". Instead, he asked, "Why not me". Instead of feeling sorry for himself, he got a job and lived a normal life like any other citizen.

A couple of years ago Steve bought a new electric wheel chair. One day he and his mother, Mary, were riding down the road. They saw a young man with no legs in a manually operated wheel chair going to the store to get a Coke and snack. Steve asked Mary, "Do you think that boy would like to have my old electric wheel chair". Mary did not know, but she said, " we will try to find out who his parents are and check with them." Sure enough, the family wanted the wheel chair and from that time on Mary and Steve would see that lad riding up and down the road on his electric wheel chair "just a grinning". That young man is now in college and doing well.

Steve worked at the same job for years. His health was deteriorating somewhat, but he continued to work through the pain and difficulty. Finally, he had to retire this past summer.

The company he worked for must have been a wonderful place to work. They loved Steve and kept in touch with him after his retirement. They called him one day and asked how everything was going. He said that everything was fine except that his air conditioner was broken, but that was not a serious problem. The next thing he knew the air conditioner repairman showed up at his house, fixed the air conditioner and the repairman told Steve that the employees at his old job were going to pay for it.

Steve had an old van that had seen its better days. He knew that the time to get a new one was rapidly approaching. A van is expensive enough as it is, but to equip one with handicap attachments would be even more expensive.

This past Saturday a new Dodge van was delivered to Steve's house. It was fully equipped with all the wheel chair ramps and attachments necessary for him to travel safely. It was paid in full by the employees and management of his past employer. (I love people with big hearts, don't you?)

It is time for me to end this story, and I can think of a hundred ways to do so. You know… things like don't give up, or be positive, or to always look to God.

When I asked Mary if she minded if I shared this story, she told me that I could share it but to use only her first name or a fictitious name. She did not want any credit. She explained that she loved to encourage people and to share how good God has been to her, Steve, and the rest of the family. There is nothing like a praying mother.

Mary is my prayer partner. She has prayed me through things. When I was sick and hurt last winter, she told me "not to ask God for healing, but to thank him for the healing that was to come." I could go on and on about this great family, but I will not. They would not want that. I will end this by saying just what she wants me to say, "To God be the glory". bob

REMEMBERING BILL

Sometimes you just can't quite figure out what is wrong. For the last few years I haven't enjoyed the cattle business like I once did. The work is the same, and even at my advanced age, I seem to handle it pretty well.

When I first started in this business, I was in my late 20's. Most of the farmers and cowboys around here were a little older than me. Maybe 1/2 of a generation older, I am guessing. They were my mentors and friends. We had a bond just like when I was in Vietnam. Closer than brothers. Now most of them are gone, retired, or unable to continue. I just figured it out, I miss my friends. This is what is wrong.

We lost another "good un" today. Bill Bumgarner. Bill wasn't a farmer, but he was an important part of the farming, cattle, and agricultural community. He was an equipment operator. He cleared land with his bull dozer, hauled dirt, gravel, and sand. Just about anything you needed, he would do it.

Bill had a southern charm about him. The man never did get too excited about things. He had a slow and easy manner that you just had to love. He was loyal and always helpful.

The first time I hired Bill to clear some land many years ago he told me that he charged $50 an hour. I knew that was a reasonable price and told him to go ahead with the work. I asked him, "Do you have a contract or anything for me to sign?" "No, he replied, I just want to be paid when I finish." I then asked, "Do you want a down payment or some money up front?" He said, "No." I said, "Bill, you don't even know me. If I don't pay you, there would be no way to repossess bull dozing." He said, "I don't worry about people like you." I never did fully understand what "people like me" meant.

Once, when a cow died, I called Bill to bring his backhoe over and bury it for me. When he finished, I asked him, "How much do I owe you?" He said, "Not a dime, you have already lost enough." That is how we operated. We tried to help one another and didn't spend much time worrying about our cost. Friendship was much more important. A smile and a handshake is all I need.

I will miss Bill greatly, along with all those that went before him. I will do my best to carry on that old tradition. bob

REMEMBERING BUTCH STOKES

As we remember our veterans who died in battle, I am remembering the good times we had when we were children. Here is my favorite story about Odell "Butch" Stokes who gave his life as a Marine in Vietnam. This happened in the spring of 1957. I was 11 years old and Butch was 10.

Gary Smith, who lived not too far from us, had a pony. He rode it to my house on 13th Street. David Sims, Gary, and I were taking turns riding it around our house. We were timing each other to see who could get around the house the fastest.

Butch was walking by and wanted to ride the pony. Butch got on the pony and took off. About a minute later the pony came around to where we were standing, but Butch was not on the pony. We went to check on him. To make a long story short, Butch did not see the clothes line, and well, you can guess what happened. Butch coined the phrase "getting clothes lined." He was sitting up on the ground and was fine.

I remember this story, but most of all I remember him for being the hero that he was. Thanks for everything, Butch. Some gave some, Butch gave all. bob

REMEMBERING CLYDE

I do not know why, but I woke up thinking about Clyde this morning. It has been over 50 years since I have seen him. Clyde was in my class in high school. Clyde was a quiet young man who kept to himself. He rarely had anything to say, and did not attend any of the social activities. You might say he was a loner. Since our class was small, I was acquainted with him, but did not actually KNOW him.

On the last day of school of our senior year, the buses were not running for some reason, and Clyde asked me for a ride home. He lived in a neighboring town and some of us piled into my VW, and we were heading to Conover to take Clyde home.

At the time, Interstate 40 was built but not in operation yet. The exit/entrance ramps were blocked, but you could drive around the barricades and ride on the new interstate. In fact, we would go there often to drag race. Clyde told me to get on the interstate and after about a mile, he asked me to stop. He jumped out of the car and ran up the bank on the side of the road, and that was the last time I ever saw him. I wondered "where in the world does he live?"

About 10 years passed and I was at a friend's house who was living in a housing development that had been built in that area. As I was leaving my friends home, I saw a one lane dirt road and I thought, "I'll bet Clyde lived at the end of this road." I drove to the end of the road and Clyde's dad was working in the garden in front of a ramshackle house... I stopped to talk with him and he said that Clyde was doing well as a brick mason.

About 10 years later, I was reading the newspaper and saw Clyde's obituary. The obituary said that Clyde had built a Vietnam Memorial at a rest stop on the interstate in eastern North Carolina and donated it to the State.

I knew from the day that I took Clyde home that he was a special kind of man. I wish I had known Clyde better, but I am thankful for the few minutes I had with him the day I took him home. I do not think that any of us knew the real Clyde.

Sometimes you overlook an orchid while searching for a rose. Still water runs deep. RIP, Clyde. bob

REMEMBERING KENNY

Another local man, Ken Hollar, has passed away. We were not close friends, but I have a fond memory of him.

Ken owned a country store before they were called convenience stores. One time after the gas crisis in the 70's, I stopped to fill up my Buick Electra. Gasoline was at an all-time high, about $.70 a gallon. When Ken got through filling my car up, he said, "Don't leave, I will be right back." When he got back, he gave me a Coke. He said that was the most gas he had ever pumped at one time. I think my bill was about $14. Times have changed. bob

REMEMBERING BILLY AND LYNDON

When Gaye and I first got married in 1970, we bought a brand-new, split-level house in a brand-new housing development. We had no children of our own at the time, but our home was always full of the children of our neighbors......we liked that. There were the Bray children, the Shuman children, the Sigmon girls, the Herman children, a little red-headed girl named Donna Pate, a 10-year old boy named Eugene Childers who sang and played his guitar at nursing homes. He would always come by our house and sing, "I've got the Joy Joy Joy Down in My Heart."

One of my favorite stories involved a young Billy Bray and Donna Pate. Donna was our backyard neighbor and Billy lived about a block away from Donna. One day Donna's dad had hired young Billy to paint his garage door. Gaye was in our kitchen washing dishes, and she could see Billy getting ready to paint the door with Donna standing there, "getting on his nerves." Gaye told me, "There is going to be trouble." I looked out the window to see what Gaye was talking about, and at that moment, Billy dumped the whole gallon of white paint on Donna's head. Billy took off running toward his house and Donna, crying loudly, ran into her house.

The next thing we knew, Donna and her mother came to our house wanting help. I remember washing Donna's head in our back yard with our water hose, time and time again. Donna's hair was tinted white for a long time after that until it finally grew out.

Young Billy passed away last week. I am guessing that he was in his early 50's now. We loved young Billy and drove by his old house last week as a way to show our respect.

Another one that often came by was a young, black kid, Lyndon Mauney, who was a student of Gaye's. He didn't live in the development. His father was a tenant farmer and they lived on that farm. He loved Gaye and didn't miss a chance to come to visit us.

After we moved from the development, we bought the farm that was located just across the road from the farm where Lyndon's father worked. Lyndon became a frequent visitor to our farm.

Early in life, Lyndon developed kidney disease and had a kidney transplant at Baptist Hospital in Winston Salem, about 60 miles from here. One night, Gaye and I told his parents that we would drive them to Winston Salem because we wanted to visit Lyndon as well.

When we got there, Lyndon was dressed and had been released from the hospital and was ready to go home.

At the time we had a mid-sized Chevrolet Celebrity. We decided to let Lyndon ride in the front bucket seat with me and Gaye and Lyndon's parents were going to ride in the back seat. Lyndon's dad weighed over 300 pounds and was probably 6'5". His mother was over 6'. I remember Gaye was crowded in the back seat sitting between them.

When we got onto the interstate to drive home, I noticed the car did not handle properly. There was so much weight in the back seat that the front tires of the car were barely touching the road and the car just did not steer properly. I remember driving down that interstate at 40MPH. I never was so glad to finally get home.

Lyndon passed away yesterday. His diseases finally got the best of him. I will never forget that smiling and happy face.

RIP Billy and Lyndon. Sweet Memories. bob

REMEMBERING GEORGE

I don't know how Webster defines friends. Most of my friends have different personalities and are so diverse that it would be hard for me to define the word "friend."

A couple days ago a friend called that I had not seen or heard from in a good while. We were outside and couldn't take the call, so he left a message that "he hadn't seen or heard from us in a while and hoped that all is well." It was good to hear from him. I will drop by to see him soon. That got me to thinking about old friends.

One of the best friends I ever had was a fellow named George. I called him Gorgeous George and he called me Uncle Bob. George was a self-employed mechanic, body man, and car painter by trade.

Gorgeous wanted to buy a car that I had, but he did not have the money. He asked if he could make weekly payments… sorta like the "buy here, pay here" car lots. That was fine with me. Just a couple days after he took delivery of the car, he got sick and was unable to work and make his payment to me. I wasn't a bit worried about it.

He was sick for probably a month, and each week he would call to report in that he could not make the payment. I finally told him to forget about paying me… he could work it off. I have tractors, cars, and trucks that he could maintain for me.

I don't remember what all he did. The only thing I remember is he put new brake pads on a truck and probably a few other things.

During this same time, I was restoring an old antique tractor as a hobby. I had everything done except the painting. I wanted a professional paint job so I asked Gorgeous if he still owed me any money. He said, "You know I do." "How much?" I responded. He said, "I don't know... I thought you were keeping up with it." Dadgum, I thought he was keeping up with it. There was a failure to communicate, but good friends don't worry about things like that.

"How were you going to know when you had worked off your debt?" I asked. He grinned and said, "I was going to work until you told me to stop." It is a wonderful thing that we trusted each other enough to accept the others word. Money issues often separate families and friends.

"Would it be fair for you to paint my old tractor and we will call it even?" I queried. Gorgeous smiled and said, "That is perfect, Uncle Bob."

Gorgeous passed on not long after that. He is an unforgettable friend... and I must add, quite the character. bob

REMEMBERING SARAH

We first met Sarah about fifteen years ago. Sarah was from Bat Cave, NC... located in Transylvania County of all places.

Sarah had a little produce stand along the side of the road very near Chimney Rock. It was a non-descript unpainted building where she sold fruits, vegetables, canned goods, honey, etc. She also allowed you to use her picnic tables for 25 cents. That is the reason we first stopped there... to use a picnic table.

My favorite thing about Sarah's business was the peppers that she canned. She would pickle all colors of sweet peppers, onions, and hot peppers all together straight from her garden. The peppers and onions were in pretty good-sized chunks and were just a little bigger than a cracker. That made for "good eatin". Gaye and I would always go in early July to get some of those peppers. After a few years of going there at the same time every year, she would put a case aside for us and when we got there she would say, "been expecting you," and then she would get my case of peppers from underneath the counter without me asking.

Sarah was a poor, hard-working, mountain woman who was rea-red right and had great values. She believed in working hard and making do with what she had. I remember her telling us that she had a hard Winter. The furnace had gone out in her old house and she heated one room with an inefficient fireplace like the old houses had. She said she couldn't build a very hot fire because the chimney had cracks and could cause a house fire. I could just imagine that tough, determined, mountain woman sitting by that fire all Winter on those frigid mountain nights with no complaints… just living life.

Four or five years ago, we went to get our peppers… the old building was there but it was closed, and no one knew anything about Sarah. My guess is she has gone to heaven… she was get-ting pretty old and her health was failing the last time we talked.

I think about Sarah pretty often. We were never close friends. She didn't even know my name, but she was special to me. She is one of those unforgettable characters who probably impacted more lives than you could imagine.

Well… I have learned to pickle my own peppers and onions… and they are exactly like those of Sarah's… but for some reason it is not the same. I miss Sarah for a lot of reasons. I think the main reason I miss her is she was what I think God expects us to be and was an inspiration to me… the world needs more people like Sarah. bob

LESSON FROM GRADY

Grady Walker owned and operated Walker's Small Engine Repair where he sold and repaired lawn mowers, chain saws, etc. Grady was a Christian man who exemplified that lifestyle. He was soft-spoken and always had something nice to say. He always looked clean and neat with every hair in place, even after a hard day of repairing lawn mowers.

In about 1979 or 80, I took a chainsaw to Grady to be repaired and my two or three-year-old son went along for the ride. While I was talking with Grady about the symptoms of the chainsaw, our son was walking around looking at things in the store... especially the candy in the candy counter.

As we were driving home, our son pulled a penny piece of candy out of his pocket and began eating it. When asked where he got the candy, he gave me the "look" that every parent knows when their child has done wrong. I told him that he needed to talk to Grady about what he had done, and I turned the truck around and headed back to Grady's store.

When he told Grady what he had done, Grady gave him the best speech you have ever heard about respecting others people's property. When Grady finished his speech to our son, he took me aside and said, "You know that I don't care that he took that candy, but I know you didn't want him to know that." I told Grady that he did "exactly what I wanted him to do."

Grady died unexpectedly a few years ago. His was a life well-lived.

He was a great friend who positively influenced a lot of people. bob

BOBISMS

Does anyone know where the saying "don't throw the baby out with the bathwater" got started? In the days before running water, the family would take a bath once a week. They would all use the same water and tub. The dirtiest person, who was usually the father, got to wash first. Then the next dirtiest person would bathe in the same water. This would go on until it was time to wash the baby who was not very dirty at all. When they washed the baby, the dirty water would make the baby so dirty that you couldn't see it in the water. I thought some of you might find that interesting and amusing. bob

I spend a lot of time in solitude. Last night a friend called and asked what I did today. After I told her, she said she couldn't stand to be alone all the time like that. It never occurred to me until then that I spend a lot of time alone. I chose this lonely lifestyle of raising cattle and I guess I'm suited to it. "Don't you ever get lonely?" she asked. My answer was, "No, how can you be lonely when you're never alone?" Come and see us sometime. We're usually here. You just can't see us from the road. bob

I read a report that says watches will be a thing of the past in a few years. It seems that most people use their cell phone or other mobile device to check the time. I still wear a watch because of the convenience of it and probably will continue to do so.

Of course, I remember when I said, "Why would I ever want a home computer?" or "No way will I ever buy a bottle of water," or "Cell phones are a fad that will soon go away." bob

Fall and spring are my busy times of the year. I've got an early start bush hogging, fertilizing, etc. When I was bush hogging yesterday, I noticed a lot of small cedar trees growing along the fence line. They need to be lopped off to keep them from getting entangled in the fences. It seems that it happened over night and they just crept up on me. I got to thinking about how sin and wrong-doing just creeps up on us. At first it seems harmless or trivial, but it can become a "huge tree" that needs to be lopped off. Let's reevaluate ourselves and lop off what we need to get rid of. God Bless. bob

I don't understand thieves, but here is one I really don't understand. A friend of ours returned home Saturday night and found that the utility room at the back of their carport had been broken into. The only thing in the room was a freezer full of meat and miscellaneous groceries. The lock on the freezer had been broken. When my friends looked into the freezer the only thing that was missing was a Mrs. Smith's Frozen Pie. They had bought three of them that week and they were still in the grocery bag. The thief only took ONE. Why not the whole bag and get all three? I guess it was a thief with a conscience. bob

Many people are naming the things they are thankful for this month. Of all the things I am thankful for, I am most thankful for the things that have been taken away from me or things that I never had in the first place......things like greed, hate, envy etc. bob

Feeling sad tonight. I heard that Jonathan Holler, the man who invented the hokey pokey died. They said that everything went well until they tried to put him in the casket. It seems they put his right leg in and everything went downhill from there. bob

Gaye has gone to the beach for a few days and I have decided to take a little R&R myself. I ran a few errands and had wings for lunch. Everywhere I went people were thanking me for my service. I appreciate all those thoughts and well wishes, but Lord knows that just having the honor to serve is all the thanks that I need. bob

I had a good laugh this morning. I decided to put on a jacket for the first time that someone gave me for Christmas. It was surprising to learn that it is a lady's jacket. The lady who gave it to me is notorious for re-gifting. Heck, I don't mind wearing a lady's jacket, but those lefthanded zippers are hard to get used to.

Do you know why lady's blouses and jackets are buttoned opposite from men's? Well, I will tell you anyway. In the early days, affluent folks had employees who worked in their home to help the young girls get dressed. It was easier for them to button the blouse as they faced the child.

I know you are thrilled to know that. bob

Something happened to me today that I'll bet has never happened to any of you. I got passed by a moped. The truth is I was on a tractor going about 10 MPH. To add insult to injury, when the drunk got beside of me he looked at me and grinned. I guess he was jubilated for passing someone for the first time. I caught up with him at the stop sign at Oxford Baptist Church. I had the hay spear attached to the frontend loader and felt like sticking it in his exhaust pipe (or worse) and picking him up, but I thought better of it. bob

One of my favorite things is to sit on my porch at night and ponder things. Sometimes it is serious things...sometimes it is foolishness. Tonight, I am thinking about all of the division in the world... politics, churches, families, employees/employer's etc. You get the picture. I think division is the biggest threat to America. I wish I knew a way to bring unity. Maybe if I bought the world a Coke it would help. bob

I was in town today to get my allergy medicine at H & W Drug. After eating a homemade chicken salad, pimento cheese, and egg salad combination plate, I decided to go to High Lite's lady's store on the corner and buy something for Gaye. I noticed a pair of black slacks with a blue top in the window and told Irene, the store manager, that I wanted that. Irene told me "No, that Gaye would not like that". It was not the style that Gaye would like. I told her to just get me what she thinks Gaye will like. I ended up with a pair of black slacks and a multi colored top that Gaye really liked when I got home with it. You can only get service like that in a small town. I'm glad I live here. bob

When we were growing up, Mama would take the Christmas tree down on the morning after Christmas. My sister and I would beg her to leave it up longer. In my later life, I asked Mom why she did that. She quickly replied, "When it's over, it's over". That was pretty simple, yet prolific in my mind. I have noticed that some people just never seem to know when it's over. They just like to wallow in their misery... It often happens in relationships... you just don't want to let go, so you continue in your misery. Sometime you need to just walk away and accept things for what they are. Kenny Rogers said, "You need to know when to hold'em, know when to fold'em, know when to walk away, know when to run". Mama summed it up best, "when it's over, it's over." bob

I might be a little smarter than most of y'all think. I read today that weak people seek revenge, strong people forgive, and intelligent people ignore it. I must be pretty intelligent because I have been ignoring things all my life… parents, teachers, preachers, police, doctors, or any authority for that matter. I got over it though. bob

It is my policy not to give advice unless asked. From time to time, I see a need to break that policy. I do not know the name of them, but many of you ladies are wearing tight pants that are skin tight from the ankle to the waist. They remind me of pantyhose being worn on the outside. My advice is, "some of y'all don't need to be wearing them". I hope I have been helpful. bob

I have talked to two people today who have recently made small mistakes. As they were telling me about their dilemma, it was obvious that it was their fault, BUT did they admit it… No, it was somebody else's fault. Yeah, right.

Listen carefully. We all mess up and make mistakes. That is human. When you make a mistake admit it, ask forgiveness, correct it, learn from it and do whatever else is necessary and move on. DON'T BLAME SOMEONE ELSE. Take responsibility for your own actions. By the way, everyone knows it was your fault anyway. bob

Gaye and I were in Walmart about an hour ago. As we were walking down the coffee aisle a lady stopped me and asked me if the bag of Starbucks Coffee in her hand was decaffeinated. "No", I replied. "Will you help me find it" she asked? "Yes, of course I will". I found the decaf breakfast blend and she wanted to know how I knew it was decaf. " Because it says decaf in the upper left corner', I explained. "Are you sure" she queried, decaf has two F's." I told her decaffeinated had two F's but the abbreviation only had one. "Are you sure and how do you know", she questioned? "Because I'm smart and I just know", I jokingly replied. She thanked me and went on her way. When she got to the end of the aisle, she turned, and with a big grin, yelled " You are smart," and she was gone, never to be seen again. bob

Life is not about the number of breaths you take... but, rather, those moments that take your breath away. I have had plenty.

Most of you think I am referring to those magic, breathless moments that you share with a loved one... and I am.

Also... Remember those scary, unpleasant, and tense moments that took your breath away. I remember getting shot at, an airplane crash landing, rocket and mortar attacks, the Tet offensive, sickness and death in the family, public speaking for the first time, a bully picking on me when I was young etc.

Those breathless moments can be positive or negative and affect you for the rest of your life depending on how you face them. Face life and uncertain times with courage, dignity, and integrity. bob

I stopped at the store to get a cup of coffee. As the cashier was getting ready to ring me up, the manager saw me and said, "His coffee is on me today and give him an apple turnover, he's my favorite customer." You do not have any idea how much that meant to me.

Nothing makes my day like seeing someone do a random act of kindness. It is very hard for me to accept things from people, but I just smiled and said, "Thank you." I do not know why it is easier to give than receive. We all need to work on being good receivers as well as good givers. bob

I ran into an old friend that I haven't seen in 35 or 40 years this morning. He said that he had been retired for a couple of years and he was not happy at all with retirement. "What do you do all day?" I asked. "Nuthin," he answered. I replied with the old saying, "You can't catch any fish if you don't go fishing." He stared at me for 4 or 5 seconds and finally said, "I don't like to fish." He just didn't get it. I will draw him a picture if I ever see him again. Always remember, you can't always be happy because happiness depends on circumstances. But… you can always be joyful because that comes from God. bob

I spend too much time thinking about our young people and their future. I heard a statistic today that 75% of our young people drop out of church by the time they are 25. It got me to thinking and trying to figure out why. It is because they are confused. They hear one thing from Mama and Daddy at the house, they hear another thing at the schoolhouse, they hear another thing at the church house, and they hear another thing from the White House. Ain't no wonder they are confused. bob

The doctor told me that my allergies had worsened and I now have a sinus infection. He prescribed an antibiotic. While I was waiting for the pharmacist to get my medicine ready, I was talking to a young man, probably in his early 20's, about his new girlfriend. He told me that he had been talking to her for several months. He finally got around to asking her out. They go out this coming Wednesday night for the first time. He was telling me "how much in love" he already is. I told him that "love is like frying bacon naked… it smells good but you have to be careful because sometimes you get burned." He said that he wasn't worried about that because he fried his bacon in the microwave. Some people just don't understand me and my good intentions. bob

We all have things in our lives that we consider very important. In fact, sometimes those things can become like an idol to us. It could be a car, a guitar, money, computer, a fine bull, a club membership… just anything. In other words, we worship these things and can put them first in our lives if we are not careful.

We need to look at our ourselves and see what those things are and put them in perspective. In Acts 19:19 many people who had been practicing magic, sorcery, etc. turned to the Lord and burned all the things, such as books and gadgets, that they were using. They wanted to get rid of everything that separated them from God. Those items were worth a great deal of money.

Do you have anything in your life that you put "too much value on?" I'm not saying you have to burn them or get rid of them. I'm just saying to put them in their right place. Make God THE priority in your life. bob

When someone offers you a Kleenex or a mint, accept it… it is, because you need it, whether you realize it or not. You are welcome. bob

I had a good laugh this morning. I decided to put on a jacket for the first time that someone gave me for Christmas. It was surprising to learn that it is a lady's jacket. The lady who gave it to me is notorious for re-gifting. Heck, I don't mind wearing a lady's jacket, but those lefthanded zippers are hard to get used to.

Do you know why lady's blouses and jackets are buttoned opposite from men's? Well, I will tell you anyway. In the early days, affluent folks had employees who worked in their home to help the young girls get dressed. It was easier for them to button the blouse as they faced the child.

I know you are thrilled to know that. bob

When I got my haircut this morning, my hairdresser, <u>Crystal Barnes Pearson</u>, asked me what I have been up to. I told her,

"Nothing, in particular, just the routine everyday things." I asked her and she said the same as me, "Nothing in particular, just the routine everyday things." I think that is true for most of us.

I got to thinking about it on the way home. We do not have that many "big" days in our lives. Big things like our wedding, birthdays, first new house, and birth of our children just don't come along every day.

That's why it is important to live in the day, not tomorrow or yesterday. Yesterday is gone, and tomorrow will take care of itself. Get rid of the hate, jealousy, greed, and mean spirit that sometimes dwells in us.

This world needs a bright light....and I believe it is you. bob

A friend of mine shared this story with me at the Y this morning. It was related to him at a Bible Study last night by the one it happened to. This fellow wanted to go to the Panthers playoff game in Charlotte. He took his family down there, bought tickets from a scalper, but was refused entrance to the game because the tickets were counterfeit. He and his family then decided to go to a nearby restaurant and watch the game on TV. As they were entering the restaurant, the scallywag that sold him the counterfeit tickets was exiting. As he proceeded to whip the guys hind end, his wife called 911. By the time the police got there, he had thoroughly whipped the guy and he was down for the count. He got his money back before they hauled the counterfeiter off to jail. Sometimes that carnal, red-neck nature of a southern gentleman comes out. I think we all have it. bob

Quite often in the 70's, I would read the "Help Wanted" ads for painters in the newspaper. No, of all things, I did not want a job as a painter, but the ads were fun to read. Painters had somehow acquired a reputation as "drinkers." The ads would say things like, "No Drinking on the Job" or most often, "Only Sober Need Apply."

I had an old cowboy friend back in those days who liked to ponder things. He would read those ads too and every time we got together, we would talk about them and have a good laugh. It never took much to keep us entertained.

The unanswered question that we came up with was, "Do drunks become painters or do painters become drunks?" No, we never quite figured that one out, but we had a good time trying. bob

Sometimes I wonder if the whole world is going crazy, or am I the crazy one. Well, that could go either way, but at this point in my life, it doesn't matter anyway.

I was listening to a radio show in the middle of the night last night and could not believe what I heard. A lady said that we needed to ban pencils and pens from the schools. She said that people rarely write anymore. She has a point. I only write one check a month and occasionally I do a little scribbling about something. She added that a pen or pencil could be used as a weapon and it might save someone from getting hurt. About that time, I went off to sleep and do not know if her main point was "they don't need to write" or "pencils could be used as a weapon."

When I was 8, my Aunt Minnie gave me a dollar for Christmas. I went to Abernethy Hardware and bought a 6" hunting knife that I took to school every day. Most of the boys had a knife of some kind that we carried to school. No one was ever hurt or felt threatened by it... Now they are considering a pencil as a weapon!!! Frankly, I do not understand. I just don't get it. What is the difference in boys 50 years ago and boys of today? Again, I do not have any idea why or how it has come to this. bob

I had some fun with my doctor this morning. When he was finishing up with me, I asked, "Do you have anything for "electile dysfunction?" He gave me a funny look and you could tell that he was trying to figure out what I was talking about. I said, "you know… electile dysfunction… I can't get aroused over any of the candidates."

He laughed real hard and said, "I have just the thing for you. A new pill called DAMITOL." Well, he got the best of me with that little joke.

Some, if not most of you, will not get this. bob

The long Memorial Day weekend begins today. This is a time to remember those who lost their lives in war. I always remember Butch Stokes and Freddie Link, two local Marines who perished in Vietnam. I also remember my friends that I served with who lost their lives during my two tours in Vietnam. This is an important holiday to me and as long as I live, I will honor these men.

As my mind wanders today, I am thinking of the parents and relatives of those who died in battle. I have a cousin named Bobby Propst who was shot down during World War 2. His body was never recovered. I never knew him but always felt honored to be named after him. I will never forget how his mother never got over that loss. bob

Gaye sure is getting sassy since her eyelid and brow lift. This morning I had to go to town to buy a marine battery. She said she would like to ride along and stop by BILO and buy some of their specials. She said to give her a minute to change clothes. I also put on a clean Under Armor shirt. When she got her clothes changed, she put the collar down on my shirt that I did not realize was sticking up. Trying to be funny, I said, "Leave my collar alone... I was trying to look like Elvis Presley." As she was walking away, I noticed the tags in the back of her top were sticking up from inside her top. I started to tuck it in for her and she said, "Leave my tags alone... I'm trying to look like Minnie Pearl." She out-witted me that time. bob

You can blame the violence in America on guns, racism, poverty, education, hatred, politicians, etc. if you so desire. Those are just symptoms. The real problem lies in the hearts of the America people... and that problem is being left untreated. bob

We have been having a series of sermons about the great people of the Old Testament. Today I was glad to learn that Moses was a "basket case" in "denial." Most of you will not get this. bob

I have seen, well, heard everything. Gaye bought a watermelon two days ago. She brought it into the kitchen to cut it about 10 minutes ago. I was eating cottage cheese and tomatoes when suddenly I heard the sound of an explosion, not very loud but an explosion nonetheless. As soon as she put the knife into the watermelon, it exploded and its rotten contents flew all over the kitchen, and Gaye. Well, we are going to take it back to Gene's Produce this afternoon. I am wondering if I can sue. We are both suffering mental anguish because of this. Gaye and I have developed phobias, and we are both afraid to cut watermelons. We need to be compensated. Any lawyers reading this, please let me know if you will represent me. Thank you. I am going to have to call my doctor to see if he will prescribe me a sedative. Please pray for us. bob

"Everything in moderation" is an old adage that I agree with in most cases. I agree with it, but I sometimes overdo things. I think we all do sometimes.

One area that I think you should be especially moderate is with piercings.

I saw a fellow at the Dollar General who had two fish hook looking things in his lips. He had a thing that looked like a small barbell going through his nose. He also had two of those barbell-looking things in his ear lobes. There was also one of those barbells going through one eyebrow. He also had some little steel ball looking things going down the outer edge of his ears. He had a small metal ball that looked like a fishing weight on the side of his nose. There was something on his tongue that I didn't see well enough to know what it was. There could have been more, but that is all I remember.

Surely, he didn't think he looked good. The more I think of it… I believe he fell face first into a tackle box. bob

Gaye found a box of sterilized tacks at her Dad 's house. In the old days of upholstery, upholsterers would get a handful of tacks and put them in their mouth. When they got ready to drive a tack, they would retrieve a tack from their mouth with a magnetic tack hammer. I never knew until now that they were sterilized. I remember watching old-time upholsterers doing that. The hammer would go back and forth from the piece to be upholstered to their mouth like a jack hammer. It beat all. Many of them wore their front teeth off. I just thought that some of you might find this interesting. Of course, they use staple guns now. bob

In your own eyes, you probably see yourself as just an ordinary person. But in the eyes of God, you are incredible. As you go about your daily life, be sure to see the beauty all around you… and also the beauty within yourself. bob

I was listening to the radio this morning and they announced that in the next couple days it is going to get down to 18 degrees. I do not believe it. It was an old AM radio that I bought in a second-hand store. I am sure it is not up to date. bob

There has been a lot of talk recently why everyone in NC rushes out to buy eggs, milk, and bread at the first mention of snow. The shelves empty quickly… that's for sure.

This morning Gaye and I were in bed talking before we got up. She said, "What would you like for breakfast?" I replied, "French Toast" and then it occurred to me. Everyone probably eats French toast when it snows… eggs, milk, and bread. Yep, that's gotta be it.

I hope you are all happy that I settled this discussion for once and for all. You are welcome. bob

To the person who took the 5-gallon can of gas from the bed of my truck, I simply want to tell you that you are more than welcome. I know that you thought it was free for the taking since it was left unattended. Again, you are welcome. I hope that gas got you to church this morning. God Bless. bob

Here is a metaphor (or maybe a simile, I get them confused) that I believe will be helpful for all of us.

I have a lot of tools, just about any tool you can think of. The tools that I use most often like wrenches, screwdrivers, etc. are kept in the top drawer of the tool cabinet so that they will be at hand. The tools that I rarely use, like woodworking, electrical, or plumbing tools are kept in the bottom drawer. They do not need to be at hand.

The way I see it, we should keep love, joy, gentleness, and self-control in the top drawer of our "tool box." Anger should be kept in the bottom drawer and rarely used.

At least that is the way I see it. bob

The teacher assigned the class to tell a story with a good moral.

One little boy said that his mother was a Navy fighter pilot during the Iraqi War. Her plane was shot down and she ejected. Among her survival gear was a small flask of whiskey, a 15 shot 9MM pistol, and a survival knife.

As she was floating to the ground in her parachute, she took a shot of the whiskey to settle her nerves. She landed in the midst of 20 Taliban fighters. She pulled out her pistol and killed 15 of them. She then got her survival knife and killed 4 more, breaking the blade on the last one. She then attacked the surviving Taliban fighter and killed him in hand to hand combat.

The teacher said, "That is a very interesting story, but what is the moral."? The young man replied, "Daddy said, "Don't mess with mama when she is drinking." bob

Out of respect for the deceased and the family of the deceased, I always stop for a funeral procession... Yesterday when we were leaving BI-LO, there was a funeral procession going south on 321 and I was going north. I stopped until it passed. People were blowing their horns, but I did not budge. I guess I am too old-fashioned to function in this "hurry-up world," but I ain't changing. bob

Mark Twain said it best: "A lie can get halfway around the world before the truth can get its boots on."

That is still true. When we hear conflicting reports on something, we believe the one that meets our personal beliefs. The TRUTH is that we DO NOT always know the truth. We just think we do. In political instances, the liberals believe what the Democrats say, and conservatives believe what the Republicans say. That is one of the things causing so much division in this country.

The only truth that I personally know for sure is the saving grace of Jesus Christ. bob

People are way too touchy. I wonder if some people have the daily goal to find something wrong with everything... and then protest about it.

Here is the latest thing that I have heard. A jeweler put up a billboard that says, "Sometimes it is OK to throw rocks at girls." Surrounding those words are pictures of diamond after diamond.

Some people are complaining that the billboard is sending the "wrong message." Anyone who sees that billboard knows what it means.

Well, the protesters hit the streets and the jeweler has agreed to take the sign down. I just do not understand. People seem to have a lot of time of their hands these days. They must be miserable. bob

A young girl of about eight years old was critically ill with leukemia. The family had been waiting a long time for a suitable bone marrow donor. It was getting critical and time was short. Luckily, the girl had a younger brother who turned out to be a compatible donor.

The family explained the procedure to the lad, and then asked him if he would be willing to be the donor. They explained how his marrow would save his sister's life. He said, "Yes, of course I will."

After the procedure was complete the youngster said, "Daddy, when am I going to die?" The father said, "You are not going to die." Somehow the lad thought in his young mind that if he gave his bone marrow to his sister that he would die.

The only words that come to my mind to describe that child are selfless and brave. (This story brought tears to the old country boys eyes when I first heard it.) Not many people would be willing to give up their life to save someone else. I personally know one other, let me tell you about Him...

About 2000 or so years ago someone else did it. This man's name was Jesus. He gave up His life so that we could have eternal, everlasting life. He was resurrected 3 days later and still lives today. I hope you all know Him. Have a Blessed Good Friday, everybody. bob

Yesterday Gaye asked me to dig up a dying azalea so she could replace it with a knock-out rose.

It was a very large azalea, so I first took the chainsaw to it so that I could better get to the roots with a shovel. I finally got it dug up, and cleaned up, and hauled away my mess. I was proud of myself.

When I finished Gaye walked up and told me that I cut down and dug up the wrong one... sure enough, I did. About 6 feet away was the dying one. Looks like she is going to have 2 knock out roses. I need to pay better attention in my old age.

By the way, knock out roses are not really roses. They are a shrub with red flowers.

I guess it is time to take a nap....in the dog house. bob

Most seniors, like me and many of you, do not get enough exercise.

In Gods wisdom, He allowed us to become forgetful. We lose our glasses, keys etc. and have to walk, and walk, and walk, as we try to find them. That is God's way of causing us to get more exercise.

He also arranged for us to lose coordination as we age. Once we find our keys, we drop them causing us to get in our bending and stretching. It is part of God's plan.

Also, He caused us to have bladder malfunction from time to time causing us to make more trips to the bathroom, therefore, getting in more walking.

God looked down and saw that it was good.

Remember, dying is the #1 cause of death among seniors. bob

I stopped at the store on the way home from church and was startled by something that I saw. There was a heavyweight woman of about 80 or 85 wearing a pair of those skintight stretchy pants that many women wear these days. To make matters worse, she had her top tucked in. I am scarred for life. bob

I was watching a D-Day documentary day before yesterday.

One of the veterans, a man of about 90, said, "No one appreciates and enjoys life more than someone who has almost lost it." That thought has been in my mind for a couple days and will not go away. I believe he is right... at least from my point of view.

I have noticed that people who are risk takers seem to enjoy life more than those who take the easy path. We need to stretch out and test ourselves. bob

Getting old ain't always purdy, but it does have its advantages.

I showed up for my doctor's appointment this morning at 8:45AM. As I entered, the office manager was sitting at her usual seat, and my nurse happened to be walking by. My nurse, speaking to the office manager said, "I told you he would be here today." I was confused, as usual, and asked, "What are y'all talking about???" My nurse said, "Your appointment was YESTERDAY at 8:45AM, but sit down and we will work you in."

They know me like a book. Onetime last year I showed up for my appointment and they said, "What are you doing here, your appointment is not until tomorrow, but sit down and we will work you in." They didn't believe me when I told them that I was just trying to be punctual by arriving 24 hours early.

Shoot, I'm gonna quit making appointments and go whenever I so desire. All I have to do is "sit down and they will work me in."

It sure is nice to have such an understanding doctor, nurse, and office manager. bob

I have read many comments giving advice to recent graduates. Here is my advice:

1. Trial and error are better than asking someone's opinion. Most of the time they will try to talk you out of pursuing your dream and create negativity in your mind… If Edison had asked for people's opinion, we would still be reading by coal oil lamps.

2. Put jalapenos on everything......sandwiches, meat, vegetables, pie, cake, acne, hemorrhoids, foot rot, and distemper.

If you follow this advice, the world is your stage. bob

This must be an interesting part of the country… at least a friendly part of the country. Around here, we make friends in grocery stores. We talk to strangers and sometimes have a long conversation.

Gaye related this story that happened to her last week. Gaye was in Food Lion Grocery and picked up an item and put it in her cart. A lady who was standing there said, "You should have bought that last week… they were on sale for 5 for $5.00." Gaye said, "Really, they are 87 cents each this week," The lady said, "I know… that is why you should have bought them last week." I wonder if there are a lot of people like that???? Yeah, 'spect so. bob

I know that large companies have to put disclaimer on their products, but I hate it when they act like we are stupid.

The directions on Gaye's solar eclipse sunglasses said, "DO NOT DRIVE while wearing these glasses." Who would try to drive when you cannot see a thing… well, there probably are some… Ignore my first paragraph. Thanks. bob

I called a family member who lives in Louisiana who turns 84 next week. It has probably been 40 years since I have seen her. We were talking about changes in our lives. She said that when she was in her 20's she had a rose tattooed on her breast. She said it is now a long stem. I think she was kidding about the tattoo......just making a point.

That reminded me of a situation that I encountered probably 10 years ago. A girl who was a year or two behind me in high school recognized me at Honey's Super Market. I barely knew her, but we decided to sit and have a cup of coffee and a doughnut.

She told me that I looked the same except that my hair is now gray and that I have picked up a few pounds. I sadly admitted that I went from a 32 waist to a 36.

She replied, "I went from a 34C to a 38 Long."

I was glad to get that information. bob

As far as I am concerned, it is time for a little good news.

A friend of mine volunteers one day a week at a food pantry. He helps unload donations, sort stuff, etc. … whatever needs to be done.

One day last week a young boy of 8 years old came into the donation center with his dad. The 8-year old said, "I have a delivery for you in the trunk of the car."

They opened the trunk and it was full of food and household supplies… 140 pounds worth, to be exact. The little boy had gone all over town collecting items from people so he could make a donation to the food pantry…

Oh, I forgot to tell you. That is what the little boy wanted to do for **HIS BIRTHDAY**. Work and share with others.

I 'spect we could all learn a lesson from that lad. bob

Gaye has gone somewhere to deliver a birthday gift. I decided to wash the supper dishes while she was gone.

I grabbed the squirt bottle of detergent from under the sink and squirted a healthy dose into the dish pan. The cleaner had an unusual consistency and it was lime green… I guess it was alright to wash dishes in Liquid Comet with bleach. bob

This morning our pastor was speaking of God's love for us. He said that God lavishes His love on us. He then asked if we understood what "lavish" means.

He then showed a picture of a peanut butter sandwich on the screen. It was just a regular peanut butter sandwich….2 pieces of bread with peanut butter.

He then asked if we knew what a lavished peanut butter sandwich looked like. He then put a picture of a peanut butter sandwich on the screen with 4 or 5 pieces of bread with peanut butter AND jelly on it.

I understand his point and he made it well, but a lavished peanut butter sandwich actually contains peanut butter, jelly, AND BACON.

God loves you THAT much. bob

I am not sure why, but I enjoy staying at home more that I once did. I doubt that it has anything to do with age… with me being so young and everything…

The only thing that I can think of is that I do not enjoy being around all these thin-skinned, sensitive people. They are everywhere.

Just today I noticed a girl with an upside-down tattoo on the inner part of her arm. I asked her whether it was professionally done or did she do it herself in prison. She turned as red as a tomato. At first, I thought she was going to hit me with her clenched fists, but she just walked off.

You see… you can't even be friendly anymore. bob

Well, there is trouble brewing around the Marlowe household. Gaye has lost all faith and confidence in me… at least that is the way it seems to me.

I decided to take a break from a painting that I am working on and have a little salsa. Yesterday a case of my favorite Country Classic Sweet Heat Salsa arrived that I ordered last week. I was rarin' to get into it.

We were out of the Frito Scoops that I like. I told Gaye that I was going to run up to the Dollar General Store on 16 to get some and also some Kellogg's Frosted Flakes. Gaye said, "Get me a chunk of Velveeta Cheese while you are out… No, I had better go with you because you can't remember all three things."

I get no respect. bob

"The bad that men do lives with them and the good is oft interred with their bones."

My senior year in high school in 1963/64 our English/Literature teacher, Miss Mary Catherine Shivers, had the good sense to require us to read a couple of Shakespeare's works… Julius Caesar and Macbeth. As dumb as I was, graduating academically 105 out of 108, I loved the works of Shakespeare.

The quote in the first sentence of this post from Anthony (I believe) in Julius Caesar always piqued my interest. I don't know why I have remembered it all these years. I have often thought of that quote because it was true then… and still rings true today. bob

A man got into a knife fight with another man outside a bar one night in the alley. He was jailed for aggravated assault. The next morning his lawyer stopped by the jail to confer with his client.

The lawyer asked, "I have good news and bad news, what do you want first?" The inmate replied, "Well....give me the bad news first." The lawyer answered, "They have completed the blood tests, and your DNA is all over everything... There is no doubt it was you."

The inmate asked, "What's the good news then?" The lawyer responded, "Your cholesterol level is 130." bob

I do not understand why so many people got angry with me this morning. Some even yelled and cussed.

When I called you at 2AM to make sure you were awake to set you clock forward, I meant it as a public service. It makes no sense to me why some would not appreciate that kind gesture on my part.

I just don't understand people anymore. No more Mr. Nice Guy. bob

The people who have to make the decision to call school off, release the children early, or have a delay cannot win for losing. I feel for them. I really do. I'm glad it ain't me. bob

Not only do crazy things happen to me, they also happen to my friends.

A friend of mine was keeping her son's dog while he was out of state at a funeral. She was keeping the dog in her fenced in backyard... lo and behold, the dog went missing. It had dug under the fence. Knowing that her son would really be distraught if the dog was lost... her husband got in his truck and was driving around the area looking for it.

He soon saw the dog in someone's yard. He opened his truck door, called the dog by name, and it came a'runnin and jumped into his truck.

When he got home.... well.... his son's dog had returned.

He hurriedly took the "stolen" dog back to where he got it. The owner was waiting in the yard and had already called the police.

My friend had some 'splaining to do, but he was not charged with anything. bob

Practice does not make perfect. Perfect practice makes perfect. bob

There just ain't much honor any more...

Gaye and I left out early this morning to visit an old friend that we haven't seen in a long time. She is 94 years old and doing just great.

We have a long driveway and, lo and behold, someone dumped 35 or 40 tires at the end of it last night.

We are not angry, or even upset. It is a shame that someone has no more pride in themselves to do something like that.

Oh, well. People used to drop off dogs for us to look after... now it is tires.

I truly feel sorry for this poor, pitiful person who has no character at all.

Hope my readers all have a good day. Something like this will not hurt mine. bob

Vacation time is here and many of us will be going to the beach. When you go to the beach, do just that... go to the **BEACH**. Don't go into the ocean. A shark might eat you... and it will be YOUR fault. Think about this....

If a chicken comes into my house, what happens... I eat it. If a pig comes into my house, what happens... I have BBQ. If an intruder enters my home, I shoot him.

The ocean is the shark's home. Therefore, you are invading its territory... Guess what happens??? You guessed it. You get eaten. bob

We are fortunate to have a wide variety of friends... rich, poor, old, young, famous, not so famous etc. Just about anything you can think of.

I love you all, but I believe my favorites are the senior citizens who struggle a little bit as they try to make it on Social Security. They are usually very sincere and forthright and exhibit a great attitude with no complaining.

This morning one of them called and said she did not have water this morning. She wanted to know if I would check it out for them. Of course, I will do whatever is necessary to make sure she gets water as quickly as possible.

After all, her last statement to me was, "I need it fixed by Saturday so we can take a bath." Ahhhh... those Saturday night baths... bob

Here are the things on my mind today.

Southern phrases and idioms are sometimes confusing. They are used from the most uneducated southerners to the PHD's. This is a funny thing that Gaye and I were laughing about this morning.

This happened at our son's wedding. After the wedding and the meal, the gala was ready to begin. My nephew, Michael Newton, asked a girl to dance. Instead of saying yes or no, she responded, "I don't care if I do." He later came to me laughing and acting confused. You see, he was reared up north and now lives in Los Angeles. He had never heard such a thing. Think about it for a minute. "I don't care if I do," is a confusing thing to someone from another part of the country. BTW, Michael, it is a positive and definite YES. bob

A Baptist preacher friend of mine attended a funeral today conducted by a Pentecostal preacher. He was most complementary about the service. He said that at the end of the service, the preacher invited everyone to walk by the casket to see the deceased one last time before burial. He said you can say, "Good bye or see you later, depending on where you stand with the Lord." That was an effective thing to say.

It shouldn't be like this, but most preachers do not have much good to say about other denominations. That is my observation and you might disagree. Most protestant denominations agree on about 95% of things but tend to dwell on the 5% difference.

It is like that in our daily lives also… styles, politics, sports, colleges, just about anything. We all have differences of opinion. Let's dwell on the similarities. bob

"ONLY BOB"
ACKNOWLEDGEMENTS

1.

"Bob is a treasure... lessons sometimes hidden therein and sometimes wide open. "

~ Melissa Elder ~
Taylorsville, NC.

2.

Bob Marlowe is a man who has lived some... and can tell stories about his Life Journey that will hold you spell-bound. He writes from the heart, and brings the reader into the stories, like they were really there. Bob is a natural Folk Storyteller relating tales of small-town and rural America, with humor, wisdom and a love of everyday adventure that comes to those who are alert to daily possibilities. Reading Bob's accounts is always a pleasure, and this book will reaffirm your belief in the basic goodness of one who has a genuine love for a simple lifestyle of friends and family, God and Country... and you, the reader.

~ Stan Hitchcock ~
author, musician and fisherman

3.

Through his writings and observations, Bob shares his shade tree philosophies about love, faith, and the quiet pleasures of country life. He doesn't attempt to suggest how others should live their life. He simply shares snippets of his own life based on his belief in God and an inherent goodness in people. However, if you continue to read these snippets over a period of time, you'll soon realize that Bob's reminiscences are lessons with universal appeal, lessons in kindness, compassion, humility, and heartbreak… often laced with tongue in cheek humor with an imaginary wink. With the wisdom of a country sage, Bob brings his personal journey with his family and friends to life. Between the pages you will begin to learn and love Bob's heart. I believe this compilation of memories and observances will leave you smiling as you happily read along, shake your head and think to yourself… "Only bob."

~ Roxane Atwood ~
Television producer, writer, wife, and mother.

4.

In a world of negativity, people like Bob shine a bright light on all that is right with the world. Bob is a wonderful man and even better friend.

~ Jaycee Lynne ~
Singer/Songwriter Nashville, Tennessee

5.

Knowing Bob for only a short time, it feels as though we've been friends for a lifetime. Bob is just as his writings portray him, down to earth and genuinely, cares for his fellow man. While reading his stories, Bob has that ability to capture your mind and heart and places you right there, alongside of him. If he's reminiscing about a childhood Christmas, playing a prank on someone or in the sweltering heat of Vietnam, you are there… you live his experience. After a full day of life, it's such a pleasure to come home, put your feet up and enjoy reading a few of Bob's small-town memories. Chances are good, you'll be laughing out loud after finding one little funny hidden in the mix. Thank you, Bob, for all you do, for sharing your world with us, and most of all, for our friendship…

~ Katharine Newton ~
Retired Business Owner Wilmington, NC

Made in the USA
Lexington, KY
30 October 2019

56304394R00127